budgetbooks

HYMNS

ISBN 978-1-4234-3771-0

HAL•LEONARD®
CORPORATION

7777 W. BLUEMOUND RD. P.O. BOX 13819 MILWAUKEE, WI 53213

In Australia contact:
Hal Leonard Australia Pty. Ltd.
4 Lentara Court
Cheltenham, Victoria, 3192 Australia
Email: ausadmin@halleonard.com.au

Visit Hal Leonard Online at
www.halleonard.com

CONTENTS

ABIDE WITH ME

Words by HENRY F. LYTE
Music by WILLIAM H. MONK

ALAS, AND DID
MY SAVIOR BLEED

Words by ISAAC WATTS
Music by HUGH WILSON

ALL CREATURES OF OUR GOD AND KING

Words by FRANCIS OF ASSISI
Translated by WILLIAM HENRY DRAPER
Music from *Geistliche Kirchengesäng*

ALL HAIL THE POWER
OF JESUS' NAME

Words by EDWARD PERRONET
Music by OLIVER HOLDEN

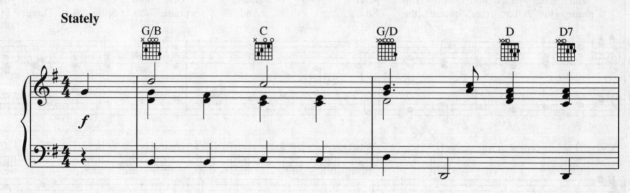

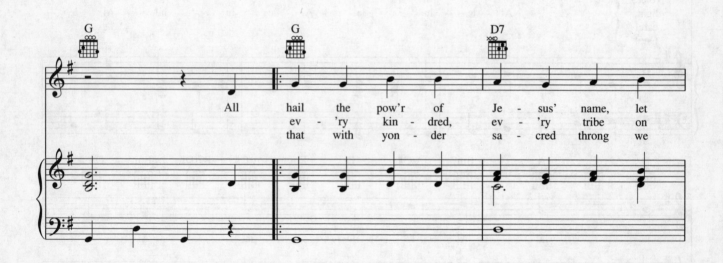

All hail the pow'r of Je-sus' name, let
ev-'ry kin-dred, ev-'ry tribe on
that with yon-der sa-cred throng we

an-gels pros-trate fall. Bring forth the roy-al
this ter-res-trial ball at His feet may fall. We'll join the ev-er-

ALL THE WAY MY SAVIOR LEADS ME

Words by FANNY J. CROSBY
Music by ROBERT LOWRY

AMAZING GRACE

Words by JOHN NEWTON
Traditional American Melody

15

AND CAN IT BE
THAT I SHOULD GAIN

Words by CHARLES WESLEY
Music by THOMAS CAMPBELL

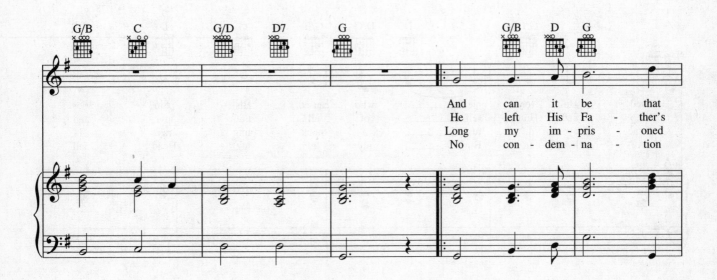

And can it be that
He left His Fa - ther's
Long my im - pris - oned
No con - dem - na - tion

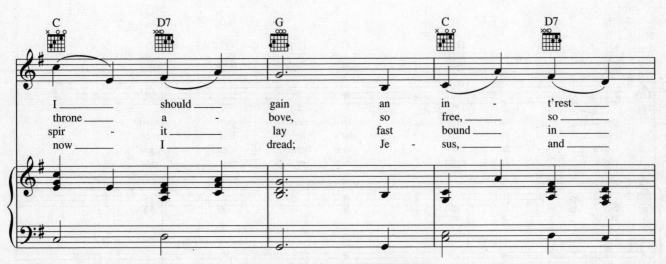

I _____ should _____ gain _____ an in - t'rest _____
throne _____ a - bove, so free, _____ so _____
spir - it _____ lay fast bound _____ in _____
now _____ I _____ dread; Je - sus, _____ and _____

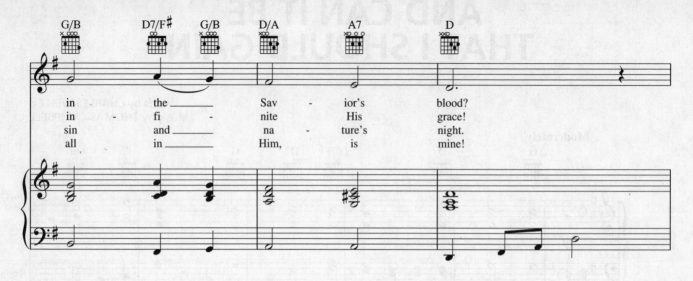

in   the _____ Sav - ior's   blood?
in - fi - nite   His   grace!
sin   and _____ na - ture's   night.
all   in _____ Him,   is   mine!

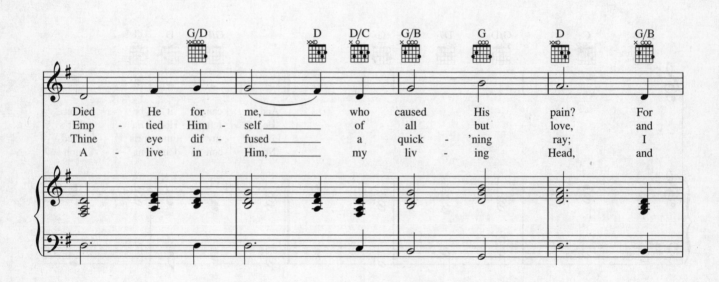

Died   He   for   me, _____ who   caused   His   pain?   For
Emp - tied   Him - self _____ of   all   but   love,   and
Thine   eye   dif - fused _____ a   quick - 'ning   ray;   I
A - live   in   Him, _____ my   liv - ing   Head,   and

me, _____ who   Him _____ to   death   pur - sued?
bled _____ for   Ad - am's   help - less   race!
woke _____ the   dun - geon   flamed   with   light!
clothed _____ in   right - eous - ness   di - vine,

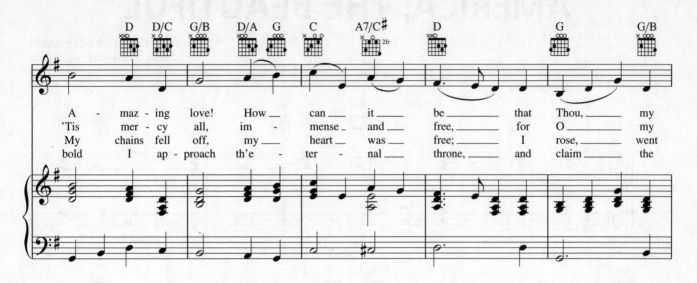

A - maz - ing love! How ___ can ___ it ___ be ___ that Thou, ___ my
'Tis mer - cy all, im - mense ___ and ___ free, ___ for O ___ my
My chains fell off, my ___ heart ___ was ___ free; ___ I rose, ___ went
bold I ap - proach th'e - ter - nal ___ throne, ___ and claim ___ the

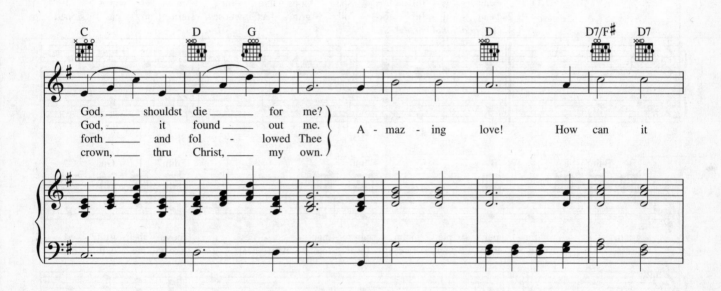

God, ___ shouldst die ___ for me? }
God, ___ it found ___ out me.
forth ___ and fol - lowed Thee
crown, ___ thru Christ, ___ my own. }
A - maz - ing love! How can it

be that Thou, my God, shouldst ___ die for me? | me?

AMERICA, THE BEAUTIFUL

Words by KATHERINE LEE BATES
Music by SAMUEL A. WARD

1. O beau-ti-ful for spa-cious skies, for am-ber waves of
2. beau-ti-ful for pil-grim feet, whose stern, im-pas-sioned
3.,4. *(See additional verses)*

grain, for pur-ple moun-tain maj-es-ties a-bove the fruit-ed
stress, a thor-ough-fare for free-dom beat a-cross the wil-der-

plain! A-mer-i-ca! A-mer-i-ca! God shed His grace on
ness! A-mer-i-ca! A-mer-i-ca! God mend thine ev-er-y

Additional Verses

3. O beautiful for heroes proved
   In liberating strife,
   Who more than self their country loved
   And mercy more than life!
   America! America!
   May God thy gold refine
   'Til all success be nobleness
   And every gain divine.

4. O beautiful for patriot dream
   That sees beyond the years;
   Thine alabaster cities gleam
   Undimmed by human tears.
   America! America!
   God shed His grace on thee,
   And crown thy good with brotherhood,
   From sea to shining sea.

ARE YOU WASHED IN THE BLOOD?

Words and Music by
ELISHA A. HOFFMAN

1. Have you been to Je-sus for the cleans-ing pow'r? Are you
2.-4. *(See additional verses)*

washed in the blood of the Lamb? Are you ful-ly trust-ing in His

grace this hour? Are you washed in the blood of the Lamb? Are you

washed in the blood, In the soul cleans-ing blood of the
(Are you washed) (in the blood,)

Lamb? Are your gar-ments spot-less? Are they white as snow? Are you
(of the Lamb?)

washed in the blood of the Lamb?

2. Are you
3. When the Lamb?
4. Lay a -

Additional Verses

2. Are you walking daily by the Savior's side?
   Are you washed in the blood of the Lamb?
   Do you rest each moment in the Crucified?
   Are you washed in the blood of the Lamb?
   Refrain

3. When the Bridegroom cometh will your robes be white?
   Are you washed in the blood of the Lamb?
   Will your soul be ready for the mansions bright,
   And be washed in the blood of the Lamb?
   Refrain

4. Lay aside the garments that are stained with sin,
   And be washed in the blood of the Lamb;
   There's a fountain flowing for the soul unclean,
   O be washed in the blood of the Lamb!
   Refrain

AT CALVARY

Words by WILLIAM R. NEWELL
Music by DANIEL B. TOWNER

1. Years I spent in van-i-ty and pride,
2.-4. *(See additional verses)*

Car — ing not my Lord was cru-ci-fied, Know — ing not it was for

me He died On Cal-va-ry.

Mer - cy there was great, and grace was free; Par - don there was mul - ti -

plied to me; There my bur - dened soul found lib - er - ty At

Cal - va - ry. ry.

Additional Verses

2. By God's Word at last my sin I learned;
Then I trembled at the law I'd spurned,
Till my guilty soul imploring turned To Calvary.
Refrain

3. Now I've giv'n to Jesus ev'rything,
Now I gladly own Him as my King,
Now my raptured soul can only sing Of Calvary.
Refrain

4. Oh, the love that drew salvation's plan!
Oh, the grace that bro't it down to man!
Oh, the mighty gulf that God did span At Calvary.
Refrain

AT THE CROSS

Words by ISAAC WATTS and RALPH E. HUDSON
Music by RALPH E. HUDSON

1. A-

las! and did my Sav - ior bleed? And did my Sov - reign
2. it for crimes that I have done He groaned up - on the
3. might the sun in dark - ness hole And shut His glo - ries
4. drops of grief can ne'er re - pay the debt of love I

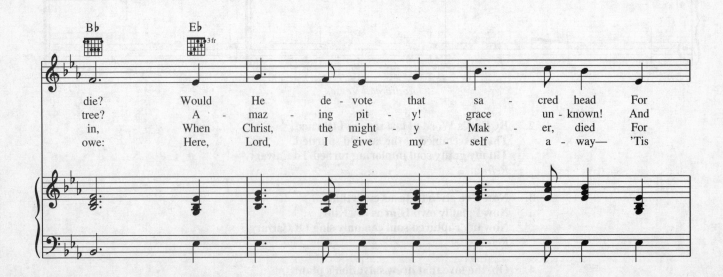

die? Would He de - vote that sa - cred head For
tree? A - maz - ing pit - y! grace un - known! For And
in, When Christ, the might - y Mak - er, died For
owe: Here, Lord, I give my - self a - way— 'Tis

BATTLE HYMN OF THE REPUBLIC

Words by JULIA WARD HOWE
Music by WILLIAM STEFFE

1. Mine eyes have seen the glo - ry of the com - ing of the Lord. He is
2. seen him in the watch-fires of the hun - dred cir - cling camps. They have
3.-5. *(See additional verses)*

tramp - ling out the vin - tage where the grapes of wrath are stored. He hath
build - ed Him an al - tar in the eve - ning dews and damps. I have

loos'd the fate - ful light - ning of His ter - ri - ble swift sword. His
read His right - eous sen - tence by the dim and flar - ing lamps. His

Additional Verses

3. I have read a fiery gospel writ in burnished rows of steel.
   As ye deal with my contempters, so with you my grace shall deal.
   Let the hero born of woman crush the serpent with his heel,
   Since God is marching on.
   Refrain

4. He has sounded forth the trumpet that shall never call retreat
   He is sifting out the hearts of men before His judgement seat.
   O be swift, my soul, to answer Him, be jubilant, my feet.
   Our God is marching on.
   Refrain

5. In the beauty of the lilies, Christ was born across the sea.
   With a glory in His bosom that transfigures you and me.
   As He died to make men holy, let us die to make men free,
   While God is marching on.
   Refrain

BE THOU MY VISION

Traditional Irish
Translated by MARY E. BYRNE

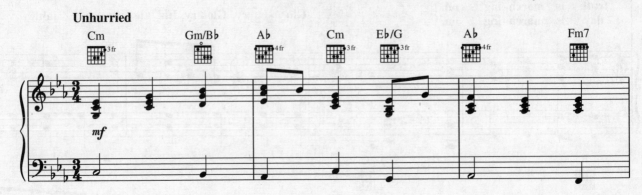

Be thou my __ vi - sion, O
Be thou my __ wis - dom, and
Great God of __ heav - en, my

Lord of my heart; naught be all else to me,
thou my true word; I ev - er with thee and
vic - to - ry won, may I reach heav - en's joys,

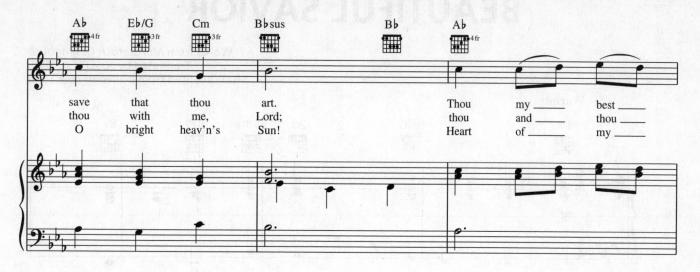

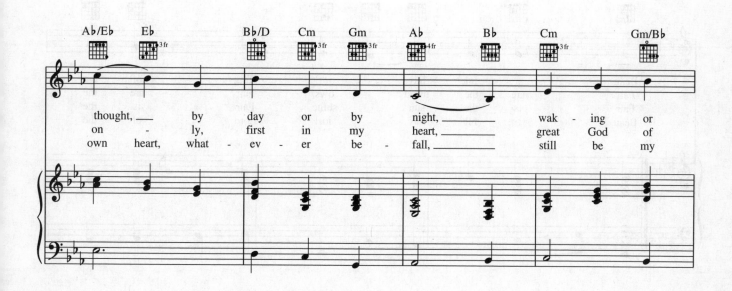

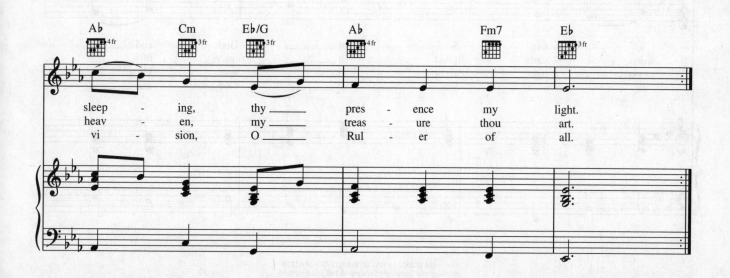

BEAUTIFUL SAVIOR

Words from *Munsterisch Gesangbuch*
Translated by JOSEPH A. SEISS
Music adapted from a Silesian Folk Tune

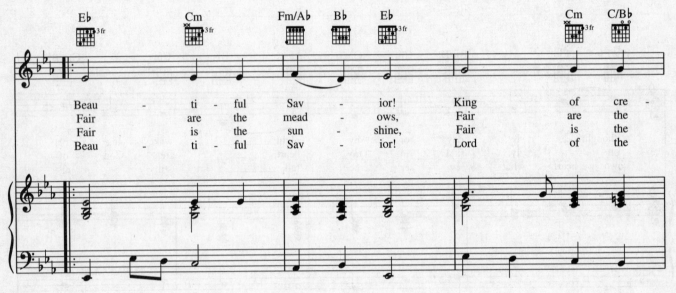

Beau - ti - ful Sav - ior! King of cre -
Fair are the mead - ows, Fair are the
Fair is the sun - shine, Fair is the
Beau - ti - ful Sav - ior! Lord of the

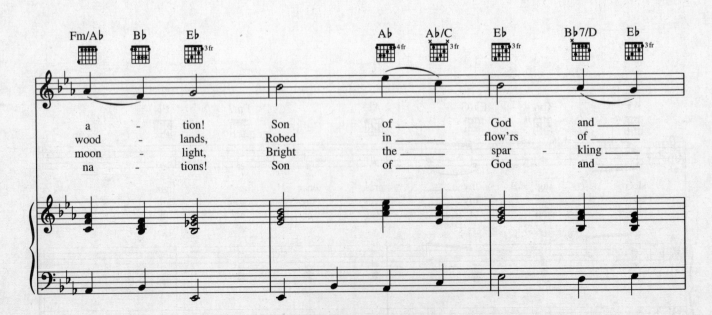

a - tion! Son of _____ God and _____
wood - lands, Robed in _____ flow'rs of _____
moon - light, Bright the _____ spar - kling
na - tions! Son of _____ God and _____

Son of Man! Tru- ly I'd love _____ Thee,
bloom- ing spring: Je- sus is fair- er,
stars on high: Je- sus shines bright- er,
Son of Man! Glo- ry and hon- or,

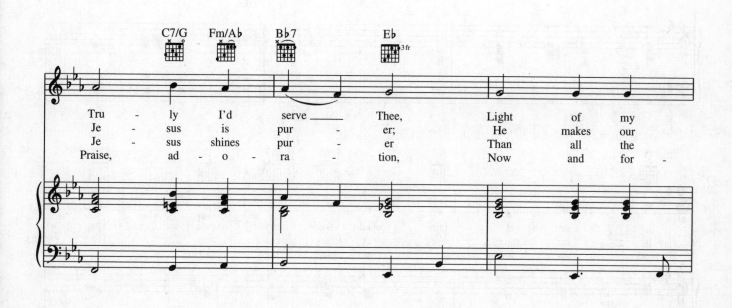

Tru- ly I'd serve _____ Thee; Light of my
Je- sus is shines pur- er He makes our
Praise, ad- o- ra- tion, Now all the

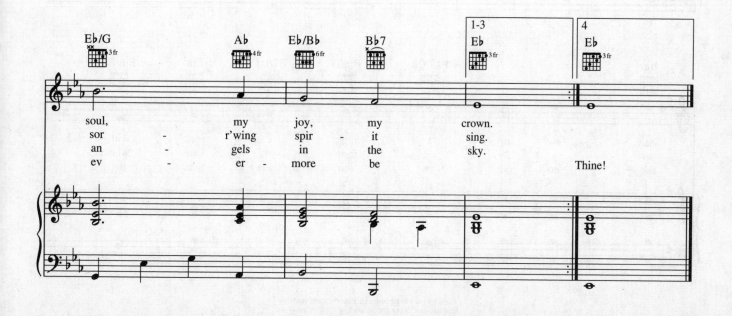

soul, my joy, my crown.
sor- r'wing spir- it sing.
an- gels in the sky.
ev- er- more be Thine!

BENEATH THE CROSS OF JESUS

Words by ELIZABETH CECELIA DOUGLAS CLEPHANE
Music by FREDERICK CHARLES MAKER

BLESSED ASSURANCE

Lyrics by FANNY J. CROSBY
Music by PHOEBE PALMER KNAPP

BLESSED BE THE NAME

Words by WILLIAM H. CLARK (verses)
and RALPH E. HUDSON (refrain)
Traditional Music

BLEST BE THE TIE THAT BINDS

Words by JOHN FAWCETT
Music by JOHANN G. NÄGELI
Arranged by LOWELL MASON

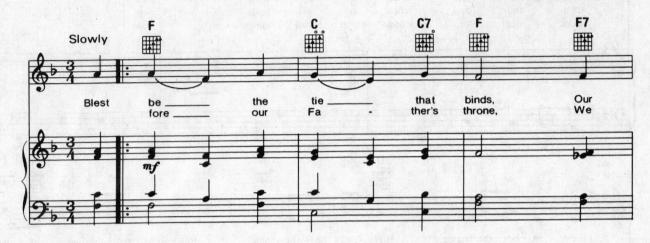

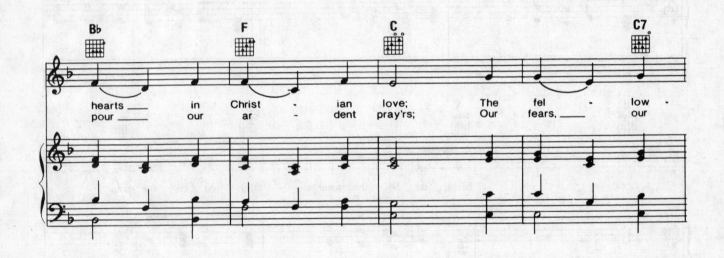

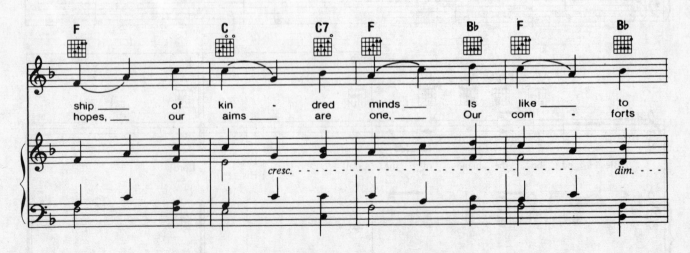

BREAK THOU THE BREAD OF LIFE

Words by MARY ARTEMESIA LATHBURY
Music by WILLIAM FISKE SHERWIN

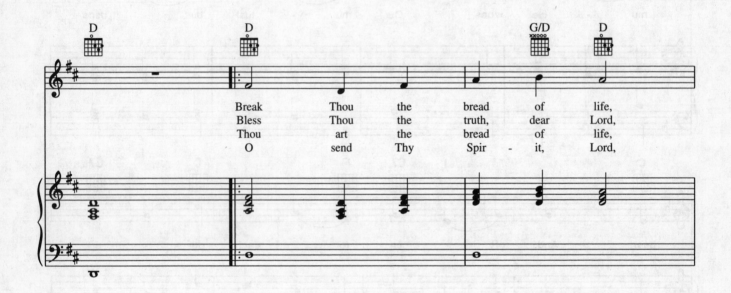

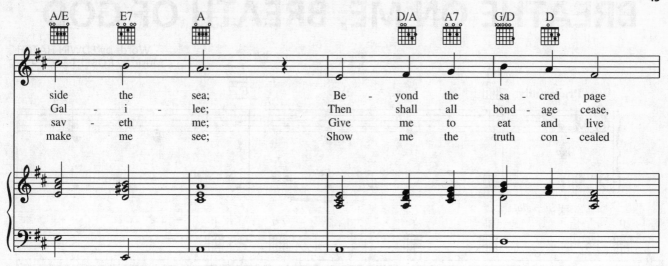

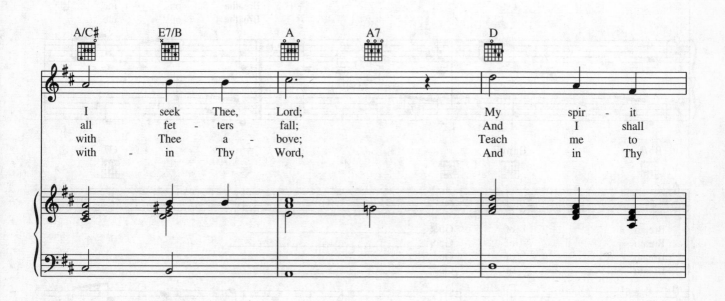

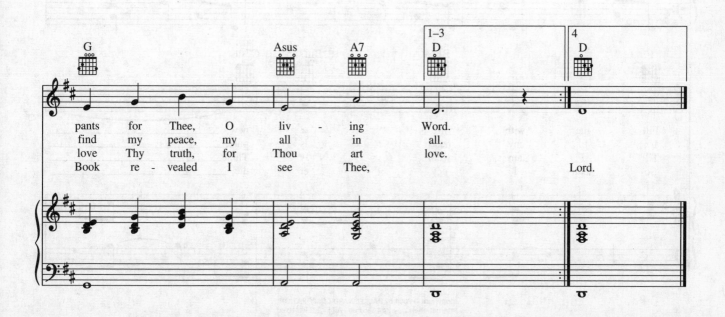

BREATHE ON ME, BREATH OF GOD

Words by EDWIN HATCH
Music by ROBERT JACKSON

BRIGHTEN THE CORNER WHERE YOU ARE

Words by INA DULEY OGDON
Music by CHARLES H. GABRIEL

A CHILD OF THE KING

Words by HARRIET E. BUELL
Music by JOHN B. SUMNER

CHRIST AROSE
(Low in the Grave He Lay)

Words and Music by
ROBERT LOWRY

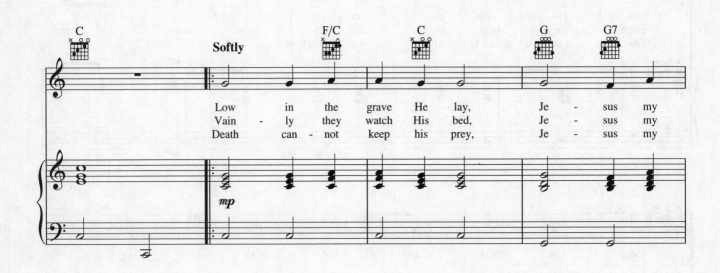

Low in the grave He lay, Je - sus my
Vain - ly they watch His bed, Je - sus my
Death can - not keep his prey, Je - sus my

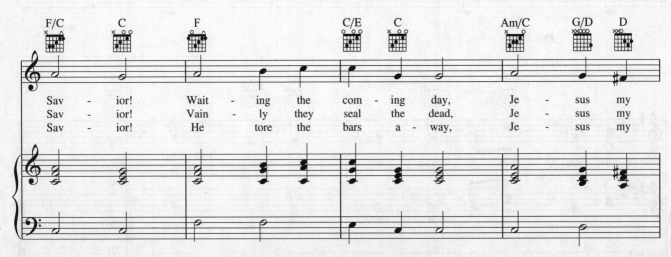

Sav - ior! Wait - ing the com - ing day, Je - sus my
Sav - ior! Vain - ly they seal the dead, Je - sus my
Sav - ior! He tore the bars a - way, Je - sus my

CHRIST THE LORD IS RISEN TODAY

Words by CHARLES WESLEY
Music adapted from *Lyra Davidica*

THE CHURCH'S ONE FOUNDATION

Words by SAMUEL JOHN STONE
Music by SAMUEL SEBASTIAN WESLEY

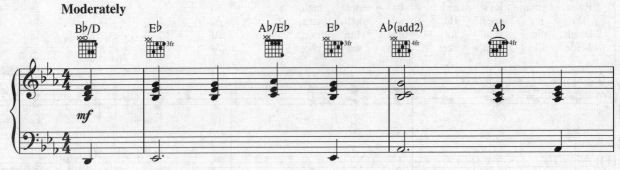

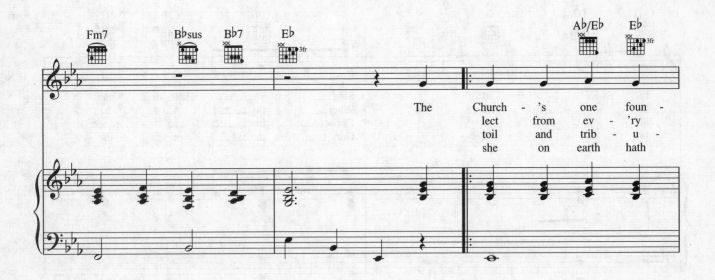

CLEANSE ME

Words by J. EDWIN ORR
Traditional Maori Melody

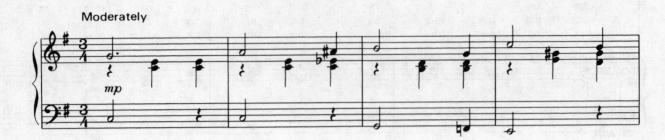

Cleanse   me   from   ev - 'ry   sin   and

set   me   free.

2. I praise Thee, Lord, for cleansing me of sin.
   Fulfill Thy Word and make me pure within.
   Fill me with fire where once I burned with shame.
   Grant my desire to magnify Thy Name.

3. Lord, take my life and make it wholly Thine.
   Fill my poor heart with Thy great love devine.
   Take all my will, my passion, self, and pride.
   I now surrender, Lord, in me abide.

4. O Holy Ghost, revival comes from Thee.
   Send a revival, start the work in me.
   Thy Word declares Thou wilt supply our need.
   For blessing now, O Lord, I humbly plead.

COME, THOU ALMIGHTY KING

Traditional
Music by FELICE GIARDINI

With an easy flow

Come, Thou al - might - y King, Help us Thy name ___ to
Come, Thou in - car - nate Word, Gird on Thy might - y
Come, ho - ly Com - fort - er! Thy sa - cred wit - ness
To the great One ___ in Three, The high - est prais - es

sing, Help us to praise; Fa - ther! all - glo - ri - ous, O'er all vic -
sword; Our pray'r at - tend; Come, and Thy peo - ple bless, And give Thy
bear, In this glad hour! Thou who al - might - y art, Now rule in
be, Hence ev - er - more! His sov - 'reign maj - es - ty May we in

to - ri - ous, Come, and reign o - ver us, An - cient of days.
word suc - cess, Spir - it of ho - li - ness! On us de - scend.
ev - 'ry heart, And ne'er from us de - part, Spir - it of pow'r!
glo - ry see, And to e - ter - ni - ty Love and a - dore.

COME, THOU FOUNT OF EVERY BLESSING

Words by ROBERT ROBINSON
Music from John Wyeth's *Repository of Sacred Music*

COME, YE FAITHFUL, RAISE THE STRAIN

Words by JOHN OF DAMASCUS
Translated by JOHN MASON NEALE
Music by ARTHUR SEYMOUR SULLIVAN

Joyfully

Come, ye faith - ful, raise the strain of souls to - day;
'Tis the spring of souls to - day;
"Al - le - lu - ia!" now we cry

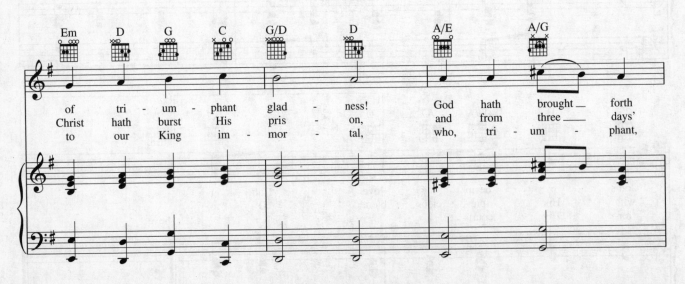

of tri - um - phant glad - ness! God hath brought forth forth
Christ hath burst His pris - on, and hath from three days'
to our King im - mor - tal, who, tri - um - phant,

COME, YE THANKFUL PEOPLE, COME

Words by HENRY ALFORD
Music by GEORGE JOB ELVEY

Come, ye thank - ful peo - ple, come,
All the world is God's own field,
For the Lord our God shall come,
E - ven, so, Lord, quick - ly come

raise the song of har - vest home.
fruit un - to His praise to yield.
and shall take His har - vest home.
to Thy fi - nal har - vest home.

All is safe - ly
Wheat and tares to -
From His field shall
Gath - er Thou Thy

COUNT YOUR BLESSINGS

Words by JOHNSON OATMAN, JR.
Music by EDWIN O. EXCELL

When up - on life's bil - lows you are tem - pest tossed,
Are you ev - er bur - dened with a load of care?
When you look at oth - ers with their lands and gold,
So, a - mid the con - flict, wheth - er great or small,

when you are dis - cour - aged, think - ing all is lost,
Does the cross seem heav - y you are called to bear?
think that Christ has prom - ised you His wealth un - told.
do not be dis - cour - aged; God is o - ver all.

Count your bless - ings, name them one by one.

Count your man - y bless - ings, see what God hath done.

God hath done.

FOR ALL THE SAINTS

Words by WILLIAM W. HOW
Music by RALPH VAUGHAN WILLIAMS

For all the saints who from their la-bors rest, who
Thou wast their Rock, their For-tress, and their Might;
O may Thy sol - diers, faith-ful, true and bold,
O blest com-mu - nion, fel-low-ship di - vine!

Thee by faith be - fore the world con - fessed, Thy
Thou, Lord, their Cap - tain in the well-fought fight.
fight as the saints who no - bly fought of old, and
We fee - bly strug - gle; they in glo - ry shine. Yet

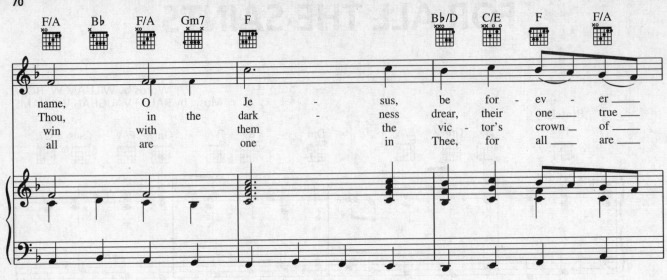

CROWN HIM WITH MANY CROWNS

Words by MATTHEW BRIDGES
and GODFREY THRING
Music by GEORGE JOB ELVEY

Joyfully

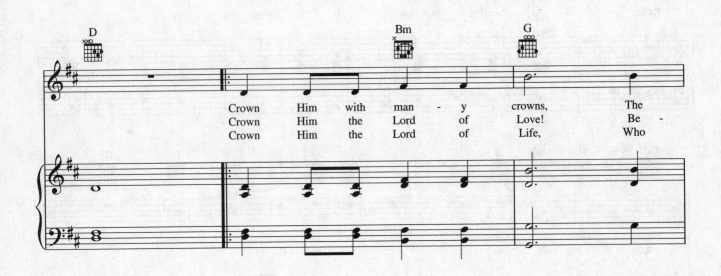

Crown Him with man - y crowns, The Be -
Crown Him the Lord of Love! Who
Crown Him the Lord of Life,

Lamb up - on His throne. Hark! how the heav'n - ly
hold His hands and side, Those wounds yet vis - i -
tri - umphed o'er the grave, And rose vic - to - rious

DOES JESUS CARE?

Words by FRANK E. GRAEFF
Music by J. LINCOLN HALL

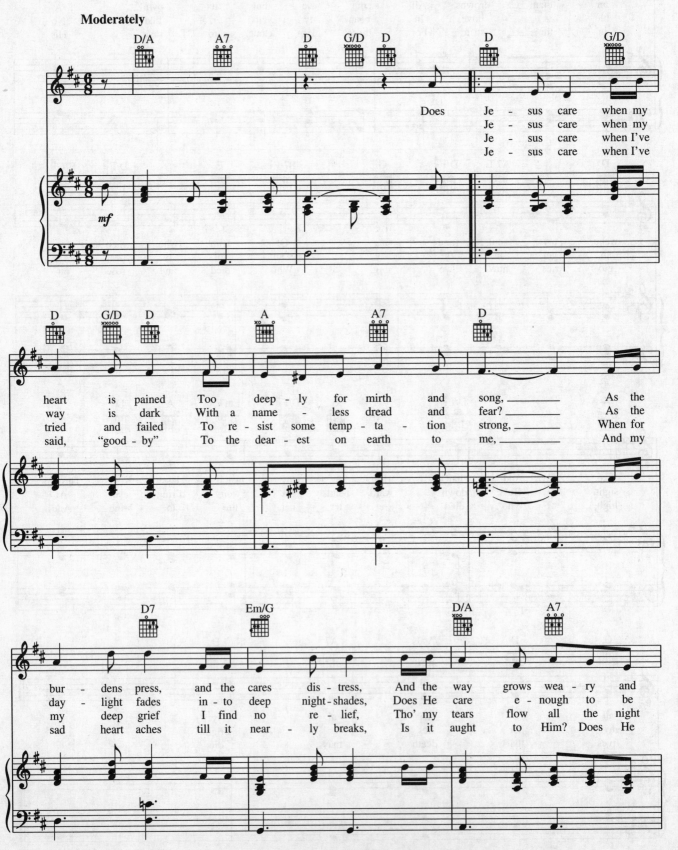

DOWN AT THE CROSS
(Glory to His Name)

Words by ELISHA A. HOFFMAN
Music by JOHN H. STOCKTON

ETERNAL FATHER, STRONG TO SAVE

Words by WILLIAM WHITING
Music by JOHN BACCHUS DYKES

hear us when we cry to Thee for those in per - il

1-3 on the sea. O

4 land and sea. A - men.

rit.

Additional Verses

2. O Savior, whose almighty word
   The winds and waves submissive heard,
   Who walkedst on the foaming deep
   And calm amid its rage didst sleep:
   O hear us when we cry to Thee
   For those in peril on the sea.

3. O sacred Spirit, who didst brood
   Upon the chaos dark and rude,
   Who bad'st its angry tumult cease,
   And gavest light and life and peace:
   O hear us when we cry to Thee
   For those in peril on the sea.

4. O Trinity of love and power,
   Our brethren shield in danger's hour;
   From rock and tempest, fire and foe,
   Protect them wheresoe'er they go;
   And ever let there rise to Thee
   Glad hymns of praise from land and sea. Amen.

FOOTSTEPS OF JESUS

Words by MARY B.C. SLADE
Music by ASA B. EVERETT

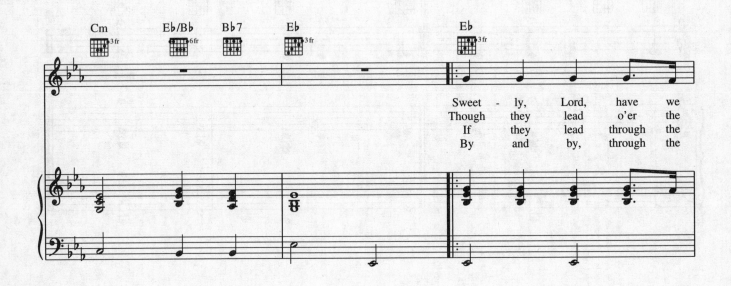

Sweet - ly, Lord, have we o'er the
Though they lead through the
If they lead through the
By and by, through the

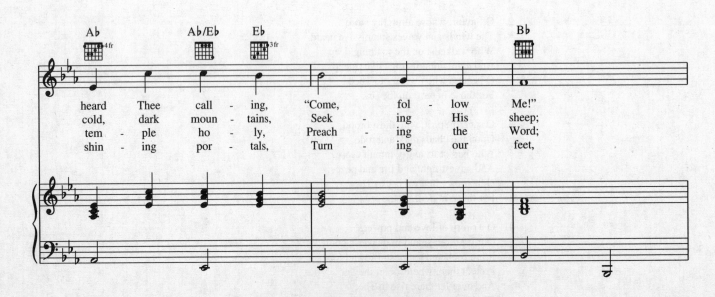

heard Thee call - ing, "Come, fol - low Me!"
cold, dark moun - tains, Seek - ing His sheep;
tem - ple ho - ly, Preach - ing the Word;
shin - ing por - tals, Turn - ing our feet,

FOR ALL THE BLESSINGS OF THE YEAR

Words by ALBERT H. HUTCHINSON
Music by ROBERT N. QUAILE

For all the bless - ings of the year,
For life and health, those of com - mon things,
For love of Thine, which nev - er tires,

For all the friends we hold so dear,
Which ev - 'ry day and hour brings,
Which all our bet - ter thought in - spires

FOR THE BEAUTY OF THE EARTH

Words by FOLLIOT S. PIERPOINT
Music by CONRAD KOCHER

par - ent, child, friends on __ earth and friends a - bove,

for all gen - tle thoughts and mild; Lord of all, to

Thee we raise this our hymn of grate - ful praise.

rit.

GOD BE WITH YOU TILL WE MEET AGAIN

Words by JEREMIAH E. RANKIN
Music by WILLIAM G. TOMER

God be with you till we meet a - gain.

By His coun - sels guide, up -
'Neath His wings pro - tect - ing
When life's per - ils thick con -
Keep love's ban - ner float - ing

hold you, with His sheep se - cure - ly fold you.
hide you, dai - ly man - na still pro - vide you.
found you, put His arms un - fail - ing 'round you.
o'er you, smite death's threat - 'ning wave be - fore you.

GOD OF OUR FATHERS

Words by DANIEL CRANE ROBERTS
Music by GEORGE WILLIAM WARREN

GOD WILL TAKE CARE OF YOU

Words by CIVILLA D. MARTIN
Music by W. STILLMAN MARTIN

GUIDE ME, O THOU GREAT JEHOVAH

Words by WILLIAM WILLIAMS
Music by JOHN HUGHES

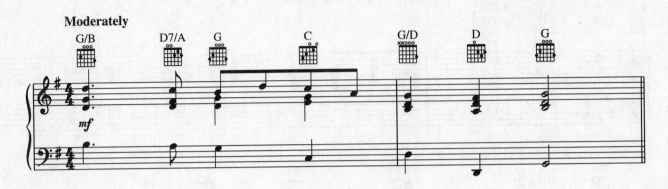

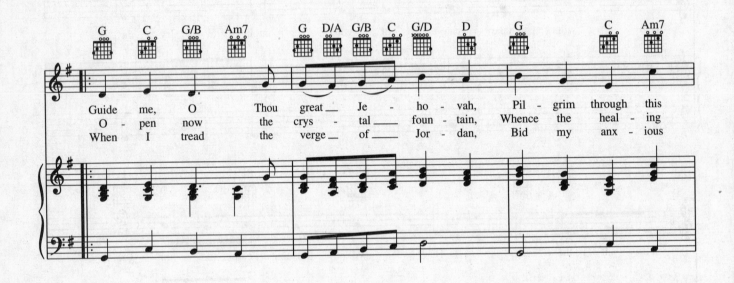

Guide me, O Thou great ___ Je - ho - vah, Pil - grim through this
O - pen now the crys - tal ___ foun - tain, Whence the heal - ing
When I tread the verge ___ of ___ Jor - dan, Bid my anx - ious

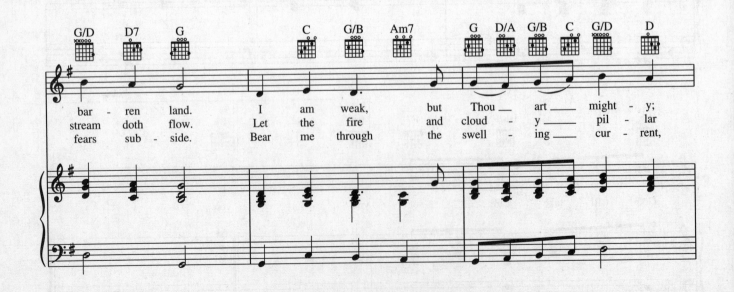

bar - ren land. I am weak, but Thou ___ art ___ might - y;
stream doth flow. Let the fire and cloud - y ___ pil - lar
fears sub - side. Bear me through the swell - ing ___ cur - rent,

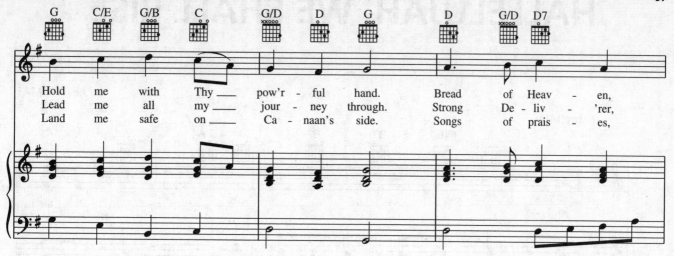

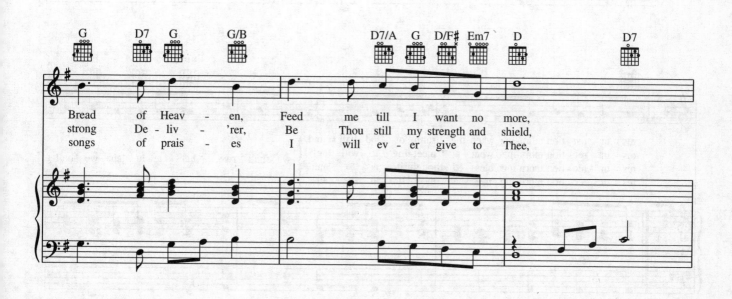

HALLELUJAH, WE SHALL RISE

By J.E. THOMAS

HAVE THINE OWN WAY, LORD

Words by ADELAIDE A. POLLARD
Music by GEORGE C. STEBBINS

HE HIDETH MY SOUL

Words by FANNY J. CROSBY
Music by WILLIAM J. KIRKPATRICK

HE KEEPS ME SINGING

Words and Music by
LUTHER B. BRIDGERS

There's with-in my heart a mel-o-dy—
All my life was wrecked by sin and strife,
Feast-ing on the rich-es of His grace,
Tho' some-times He leads through wa-ters deep,
Soon He's com-ing back to wel-come me

Je-sus whis-pers sweet and low, _____ "Fear not, I am with thee—
Dis-cord filled my heart with pain; _____ Je-sus swept a-cross the
Rest-ing 'neath His shel-t'ring wing, _____ Al-ways look-ing on His
Tri-als fall a-cross the way, _____ Tho' some-times the path seems
Far be-yond the star-ry sky; _____ I shall wing my flight to

HEAVENLY SUNLIGHT

Words by HENRY J. ZELLEY
Music by GEORGE HARRISON COOK

HIGHER GROUND

Words by JOHNSON OATMAN, JR.
Music by CHARLES H. GABRIEL

I'm press - ing on the up - ward
I want to live a - bove the
I want to scale the ut - most

way, new heights I'm gain - ing ev - 'ry day; still pray - ing
world, tho Sa - tan's darts at me are hurled; for faith has
height, and catch a gleam of glo - ry bright; but still I'll

HOLY GOD, WE PRAISE THY NAME

HOLY GOD, WE PRAISE THY NAME

Words and Music from *Katholisches Gesangbuch*
Words attributed to IGNAZ FRANZ
Translated by CLARENCE WALWORTH

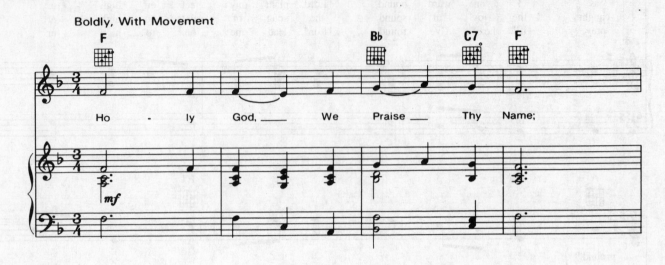

Ho - ly God, ___ We Praise ___ Thy Name;

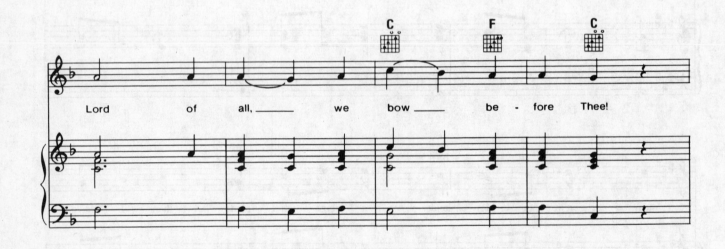

Lord of all, ___ we bow ___ be - fore Thee!

All on earth ___ Thy scep - tre claim, All in

HOLY, HOLY, HOLY

Text by REGINALD HEBER
Music by JOHN B. DYKES

Ho - ly, ho - ly, ho - ly! Lord God Al -
Ho - ly, ho - ly, ho - ly! All the saints a -

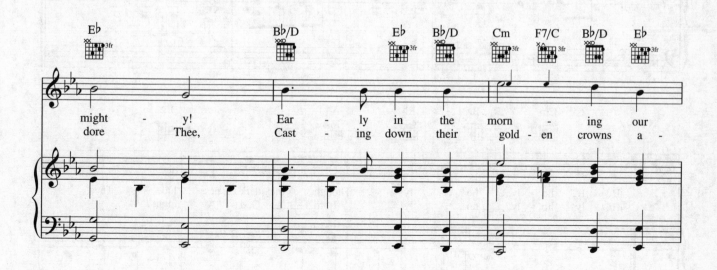

might - y!
dore Thee, Ear - ly in the morn - ing our
Cast - ing down their gold - en crowns a -

HOW CAN I KEEP FROM SINGING

Words and Music by
REV. ROBERT LOWREY

Moderately

1. My life flows on in
(2.) though the temp - est
(3.) ty - rants trem - ble,

end - less song a - bove earth's lam - en - ta - tion. I
round me rears, I know the truth, it liv - eth. What
sick with fear And hear their death knells ring - ing; When

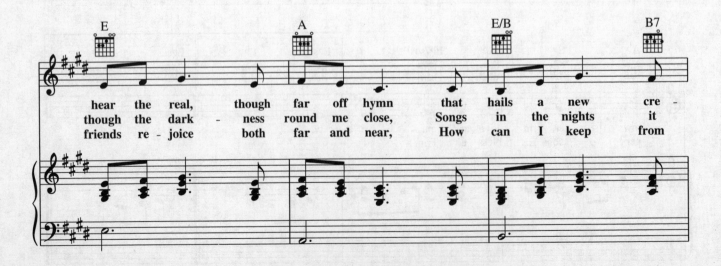

hear the real, though far off hymn that hails a new cre -
though the dark - ness round me close, Songs in the nights it
friends re - joice both far and near, How can I keep from

Copyright © 1996 by HAL LEONARD CORPORATION
International Copyright Secured   All Rights Reserved

HOW FIRM A FOUNDATION

Traditional text compiled by JOHN RIPPON
Traditional music compiled by JOSEPH FUNK

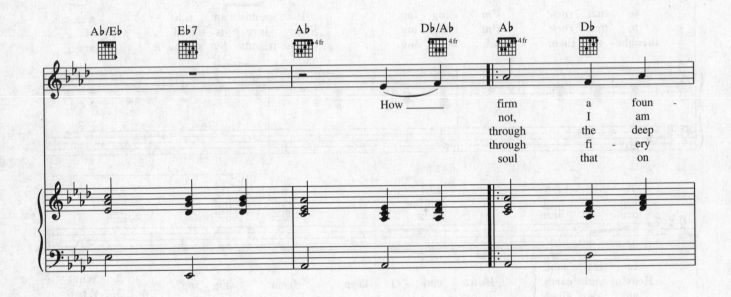

How firm a foun-
not, I am
through the deep
through fi - ery
soul that on

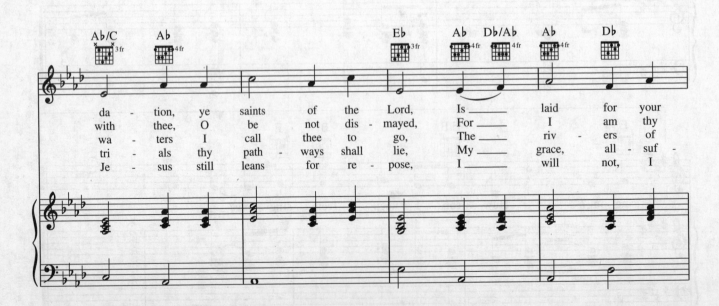

da - tion, ye saints of the Lord, Is laid for your
with thee, O be not dis - mayed, For I am thy
wa - ters I call thee to go, The riv - ers of
tri - als thy path - ways shall lie, My grace, all - suf -
Je - sus still leans for re - pose, I will not, I

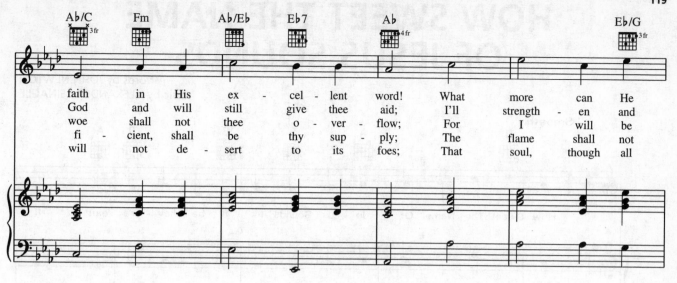

faith in His ex - cel - lent word! What more can He
God and will still thee o - ver - flow; For I'll strength - en and
woe shall not thee give thee aid; For I will be
fi - cient, shall be thy sup - ply; The flame shall not
will not de - sert to its foes; That soul, though all

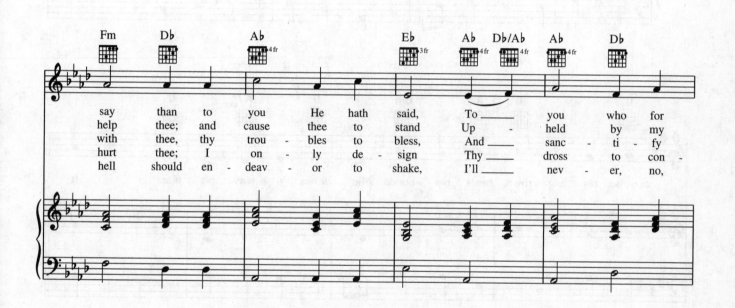

say than to you He hath said, To _____ you who for
help thee; and cause thee to stand Up - held by my
with thee, thy trou - bles to bless, And _____ sanc - ti - fy
hurt thee; I on - ly de - sign Thy _____ dross to con -
hell should en - deav - or to shake, I'll _____ nev - er, no,

ref - uge to Je - sus have fled? "Fear _____
right - eous, om - ni - po - tent hand. "When _____
to thee thy deep - est dis - tress. "When _____
sume, and thy gold to re - fine. "The _____
nev - er, no, nev - er for - sake."

HOW SWEET THE NAME OF JESUS SOUNDS

Words by JOHN NEWTON
Music by ALEXANDER REINAGLE

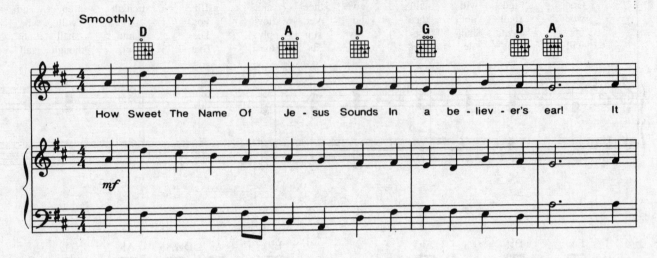

How Sweet The Name Of Je-sus Sounds In a be-liev-er's ear! It

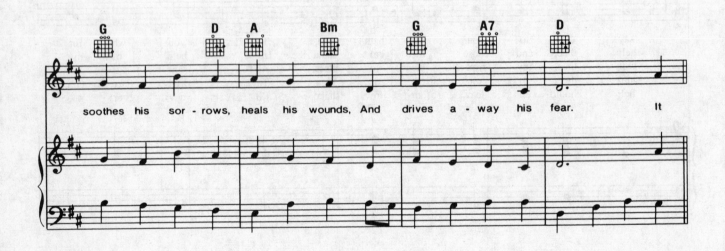

soothes his sor-rows, heals his wounds, And drives a-way his fear. It

makes the wound-ed spir-it whole, And calms the trou-bled breast; 'Tis

I HAVE DECIDED TO FOLLOW JESUS

Folk Melody from India
Arranged by AUILA READ

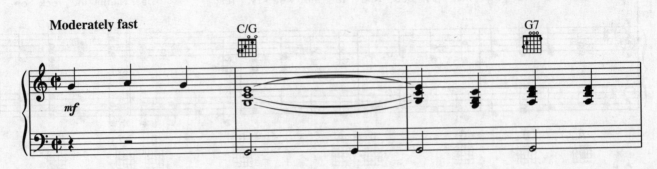

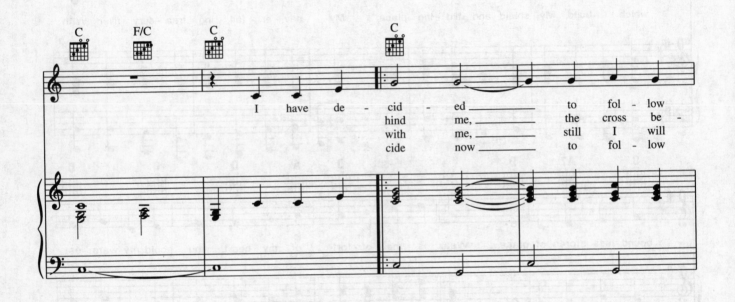

I have de - cid - ed _____ to fol - low
hind me, _____ the cross be -
with me, _____ still I will
cide now _____ to fol - low

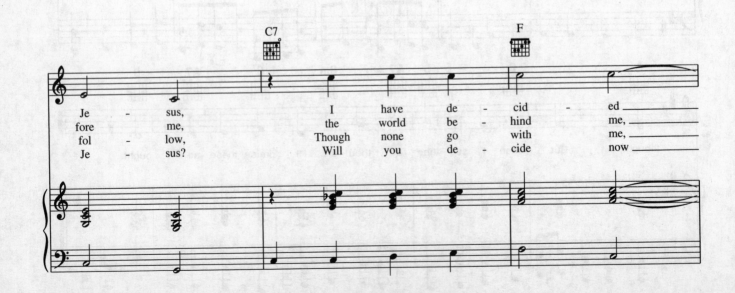

Je - sus,   I have de - cid - ed _____
fore me,   the world be - hind me, _____
fol - low,   Though none go with me, _____
Je - sus?   Will you de - cide now _____

I KNOW THAT MY REDEEMER LIVES

Words by SAMUEL MEDLEY
Music by JOHN HATTON

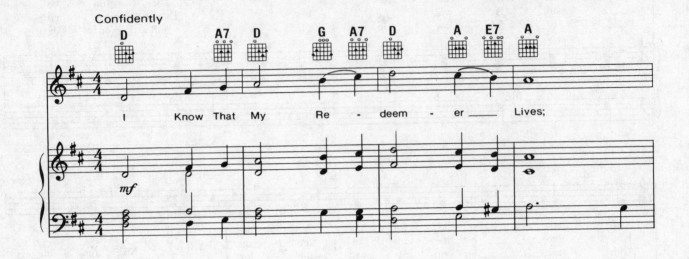

I Know That My Re - deem - er ___ Lives;

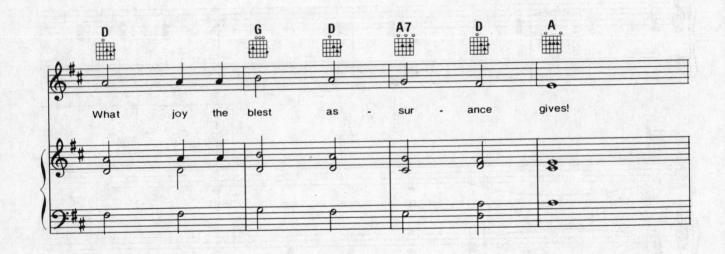

What joy the blest as - sur - ance gives!

He lives, He lives, ___ who ___ once ___ was ___ dead;

I MUST TELL JESUS

Words and Music by
ELISHA A. HOFFMAN

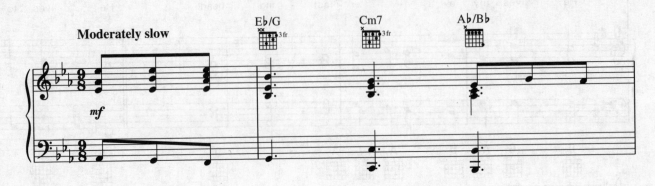

I must tell Je - sus all of my
Je - sus all of my
world to e - vil al -

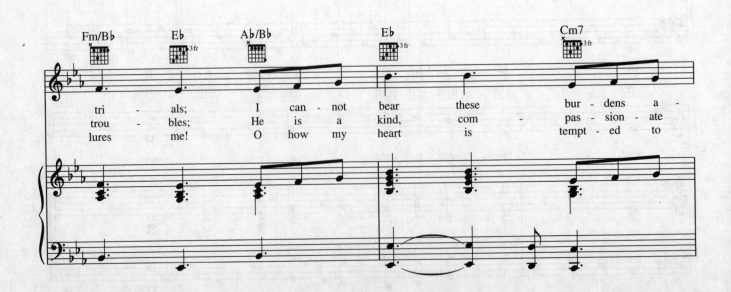

tri - als; I can - not bear these bur - dens a -
trou - bles; He is a kind, com - pas - sion - ate
lures me! O how my heart is tempt - ed to

In my dis-tress He kind-ly will
If I but ask Him, He will de-
I must tell Je - sus, and He will

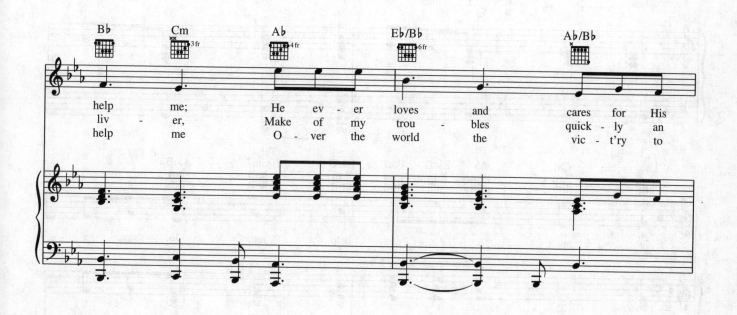

help me; He ev - er loves and cares for His
liv - er, Make of my trou - bles quick-ly an
help me O - ver the world the vic - t'ry to

own.
end.
win.

I must tell Je - sus! I must tell

I SURRENDER ALL

Words by J.W. VAN DEVENTER
Music by W.S. WEEDEN

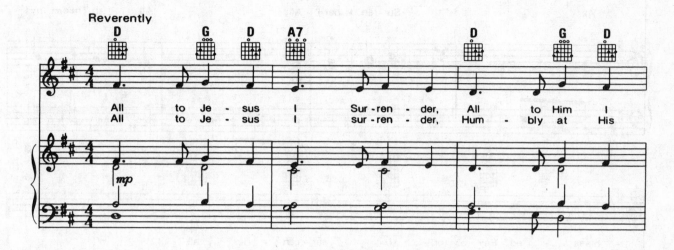

All to Je-sus I Sur-ren-der, All to Him I
All to Je-sus I sur-ren-der, Hum-bly at His

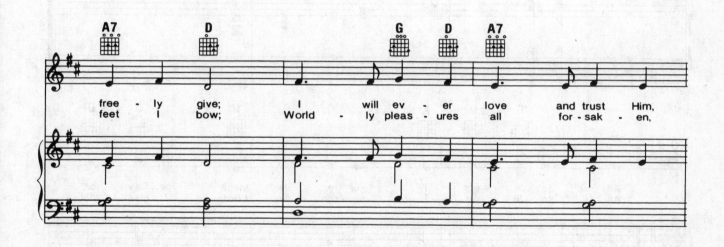

free-ly give; I will ev-er love and trust Him,
feet I bow; World-ly pleas-ures all for-sak-en,

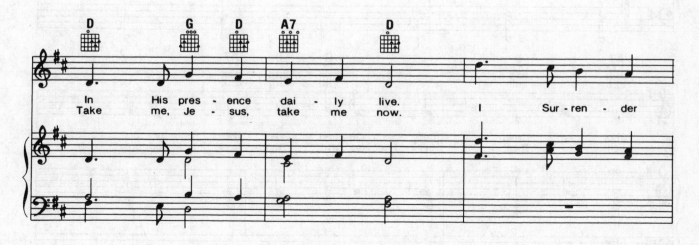

In His pres-ence dai-ly live.
Take me, Je-sus, take me now. I Sur-ren-der

I NEED THEE EVERY HOUR

Words by ANNIE S. HAWKS
Music by ROBERT LOWRY

I SING THE MIGHTY
POWER OF GOD

Words by ISAAC WATTS
Music from *Gesangbuch der Herzogl*

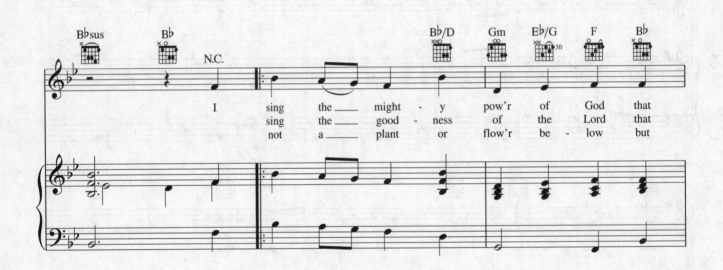

I sing the ____ might - y pow'r of God that
sing the ____ good - ness of the Lord that
not a ____ plant or flow'r be - low but

made ____ the moun - tains rise, that spread the ____ flow - ing
filled ____ the earth with food. He formed the ____ crea - tures
makes ____ Thy glo - ries known. And clouds a - rise and

I STAND AMAZED IN THE PRESENCE
(My Savior's Love)

Words and Music by
CHARLES H. GABRIEL

I WILL SING THE WONDROUS STORY

I WILL SING THE WONDROUS STORY

Words by FRANCIS H. ROWLEY
Music by PETER P. BILHORN

IMMORTAL, INVISIBLE

Words by WALTER CHALMERS SMITH
Traditional Welsh Melody

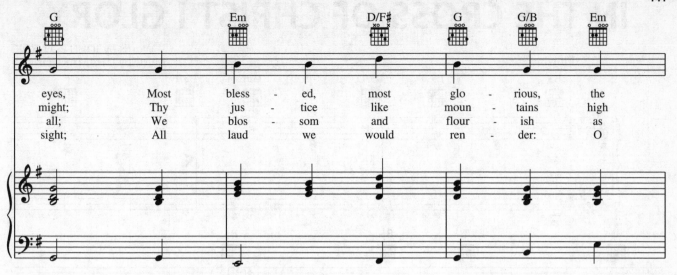

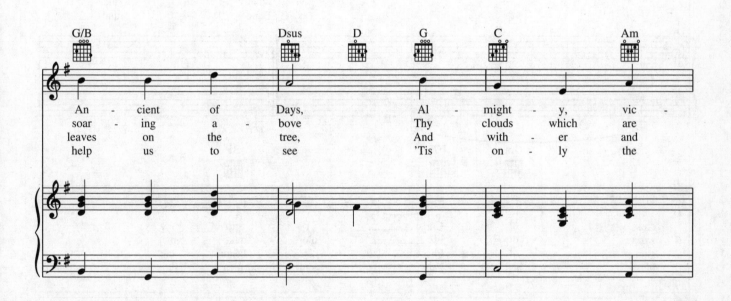

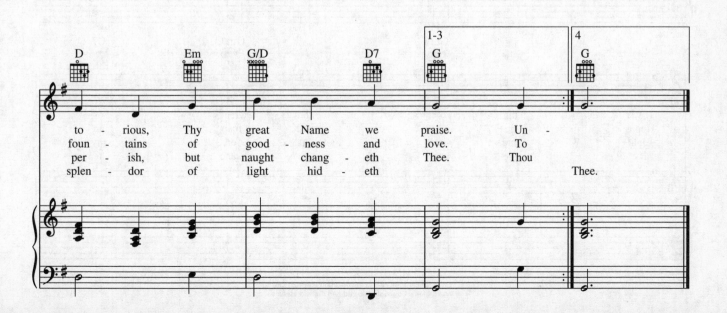

IN THE CROSS OF CHRIST I GLORY

Words by JOHN BOWRING
Music by ITHAMAR CONKEY

IT IS WELL WITH MY SOUL

Words by HORATIO G. SPAFFORD
Music by PHILIP P. BLISS

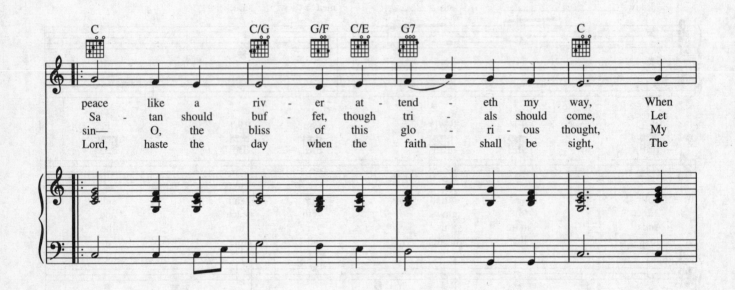

peace like a riv - er at - tend - eth my way, When
Sa - tan should buf - fet, though tri - als should come, Let
sin— O, the bliss of this glo - ri - ous thought, My
Lord, haste the day when the faith ___ shall be sight, The

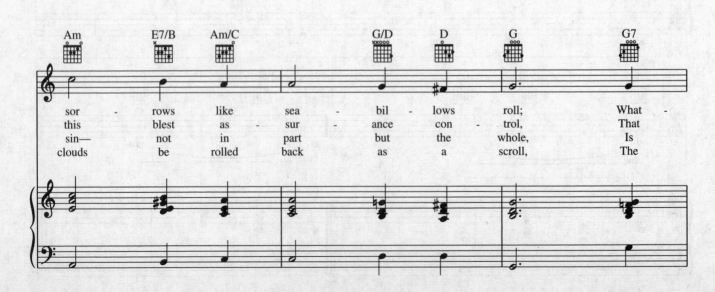

sor - rows like sea - bil - lows roll; What -
this blest as - sur - ance con - trol, That
sin— not in part but the whole, Is
clouds be rolled back as a scroll, The

JESUS CALLS US O'ER THE TUMULT

Words by CECIL FRANCES ALEXANDER
Music by WILLIAM H. JUDE

JESUS, THE VERY THOUGHT OF THEE

Words attributed to BERNARD OF CLAIRVAUX
Translated by EDWARD CASWALL
Music by JOHN BACCHUS DYKES

Je- sus, the ver- y thought of Thee, With sweet- ness fills my
No voice can sing, no heart can frame, Nor can the mem- 'ry
O Hope of ev- 'ry con- trite heart! O Joy of all the
But what to those who find? ah! this, No tongue or pen can

breast; _____ But sweet- er far Thy face to see,
find _____ A sweet- er sound than Thy Je- sus' name,
meek! _____ To those who fall, how kind Thou art!
show _____ The love of Je- sus, what it is

And in Thy pres- ence rest. _____
O Sav- ior of man- kind! _____
How good to those who seek! _____
None but His loved ones know. _____

JESUS IS ALL THE WORLD TO ME

Words and Music by
WILL L. THOMPSON

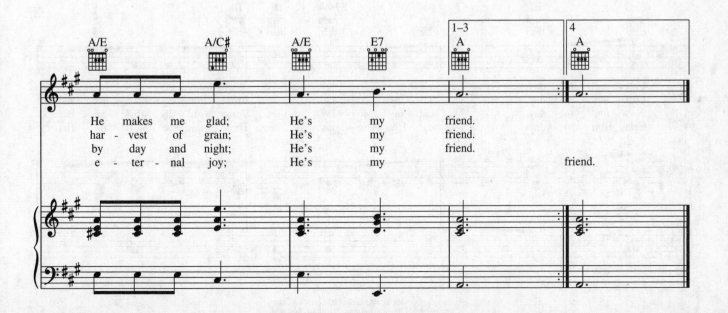

JESUS IS TENDERLY CALLING

Words by FANNY J. CROSBY
Music by GEORGE C. STEBBINS

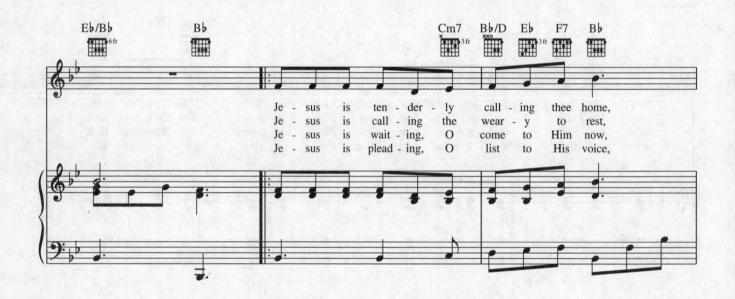

Je - sus is ten - der - ly call - ing thee home,
Je - sus is call - ing the wear - y to rest,
Je - sus is wait - ing, O come to Him now,
Je - sus is plead - ing, O list to His voice,

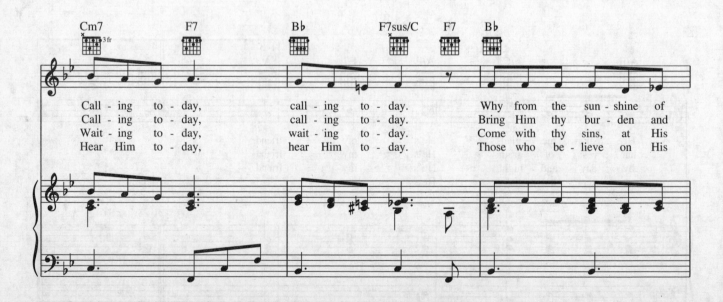

Call - ing to - day, call - ing to - day.
Call - ing to - day, call - ing to - day.
Wait - ing to - day, wait - ing to - day.
Hear Him to - day, hear Him to - day.

Why from the sun - shine of
Bring Him thy bur - den and
Come with thy sins, at His
Those who be - lieve on His

JESUS LOVES EVEN ME

(I Am So Glad)

Words and Music by
PHILIP P. BLISS

JESUS LOVES ME

Words by ANNA B. WARNER
Music by WILLIAM B. BRADBURY

Je - sus loves me! This I know, For the Bi - ble tells me so.
Je - sus loves me, He who died, Heav - en's gate to o - pen wide.

Lit - tle ones to Him be - long; They are weak, but He is strong.
He will wash a - way my sin, Let his lit - tle child come in.

Yes, Je - sus loves me! __ Yes, Je - sus loves me! __ Yes, Je - sus

JESUS PAID IT ALL

Words by ELVINA M. HALL
Music by JOHN T. GRAPE

JESUS SAVES!

Words by PRISCILLA J. OWENS
Music by WILLIAM J. KIRKPATRICK

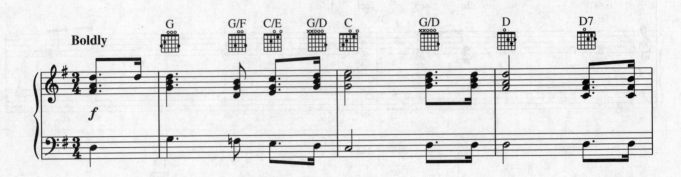

We have heard / on / bove / winds — the joy - ful sound— / the roll - ing tide— / the bat - tle strife— / a might - y voice— Je - sus saves! Je - sus

saves! Spread the tid - ings all a - round— Je - sus
saves! Tell to sin - ners far and wide— Je - sus
saves! By His death and end - less life— Je - sus
saves! Let the na - tions now re - joice— Je - sus

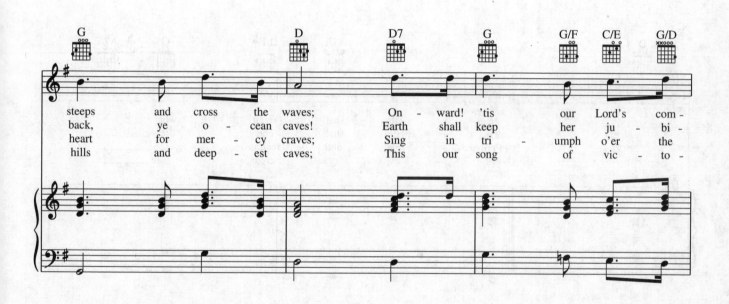

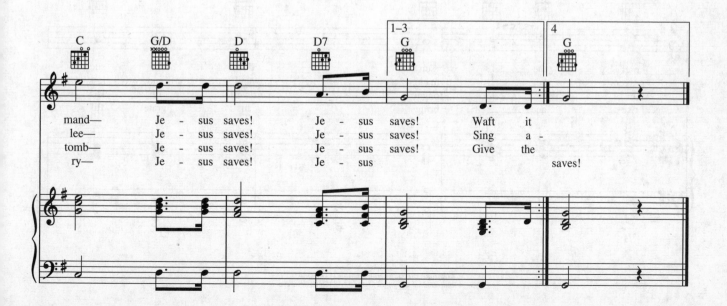

JESUS SHALL REIGN

Words by ISAAC WATTS
Music by JOHN HATTON

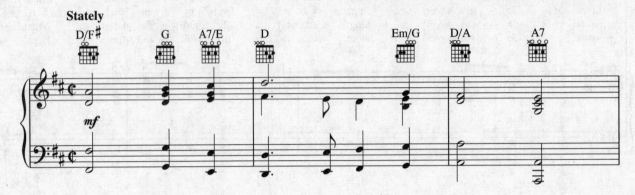

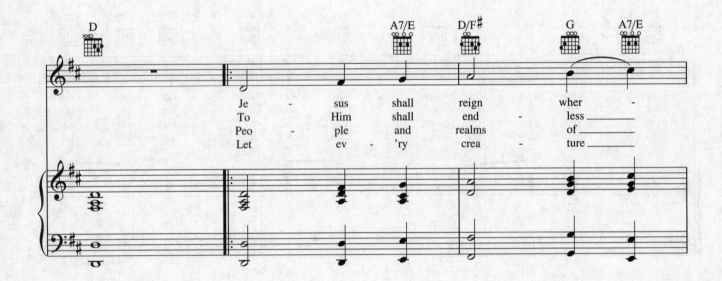

Je - sus shall reign wher -
To Him shall end - less
Peo - ple and realms of
Let ev - 'ry crea - ture

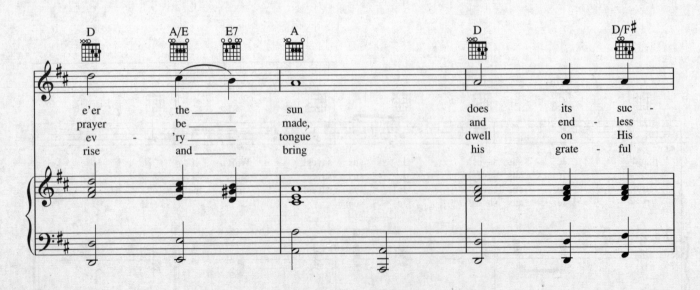

e'er the sun does its suc -
prayer be made, and end - less
ev - 'ry tongue dwell on His
rise and bring his grate - ful

JESUS, THOU JOY OF LOVING HEARTS

Words attributed to BERNARD OF CLAIRVAUX
Translated by RAY PALMER
Music by HENRY BAKER

JOYFUL, JOYFUL, WE ADORE THEE

Words by HENRY VAN DYKE
Music by LUDWIG VAN BEETHOVEN,
melody from *Ninth Symphony*
Adapted by EDWARD HODGES

JUST A CLOSER WALK WITH THEE

Traditional
Arranged by KENNETH MORRIS

JUST AS I AM

Words by CHARLOTTE ELLIOTT
Music by WILLIAM B. BRADBURY

Slowly, with movement

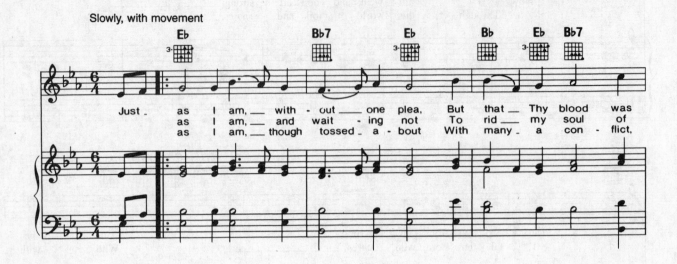

Just as I am, with-out one plea, But that Thy blood was
as I am, and wait-ing not To rid my soul of
as I am, though tossed a-bout With many a con-flict,

shed for me, And that Thou bidd'st me come to Thee, O
one dark blot, To Thee whose blood can cleanse each spot, O
many a doubt, Fight-ings and fears with-in, with-out

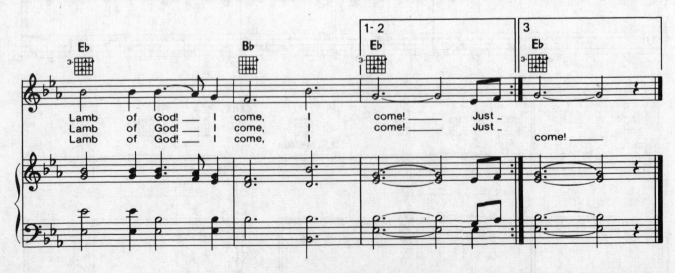

Lamb of God! I come, I come! Just
Lamb of God! I come, I come! Just
Lamb of God! I come, I come!

LEANING ON THE EVERLASTING ARMS

Words by ELISHA A. HOFFMAN
Music by ANTHONY J. SHOWALTER

What a fel - low-ship, what a joy di - vine,

Lean - ing On The Ev-er-last - ing Arms; What a bless - ed-ness,

what a peace is mine, Lean - ing On The Ev-er-last - ing Arms.

THE KING OF LOVE
MY SHEPHERD IS

Words by HENRY BAKER
Traditional Irish Melody

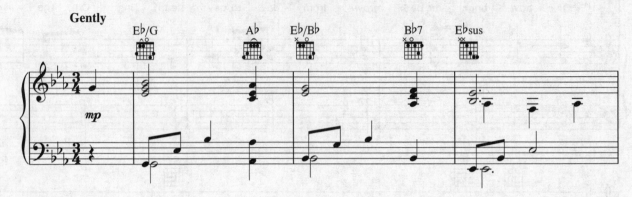

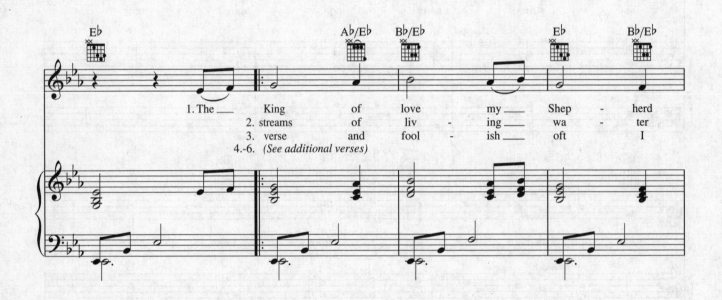

1. The King of love my Shep - herd
2. streams of liv - ing wa - ter
3. verse and fool - ish oft I
4.-6. *(See additional verses)*

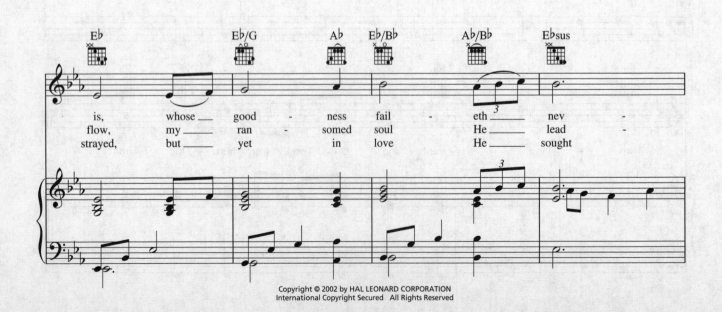

is, whose good - ness fail - eth nev -
flow, my ran - somed soul He lead -
strayed, but yet in love He sought

Additional Verses

4. In death's dark vale I fear no ill
   With Thee, dear Lord, beside me.
   Thy rod and staff my comfort still,
   Thy cross before to guide me.

5. Thou spreadst a table in my sight,
   Thine unction grace bestoweth.
   And O what transport of delight
   From Thy pure chalice floweth!

6. And so through all the length of days
   Thy goodness faileth never.
   Good Shepherd, may I sing Thy praise
   Within Thy house forever.

LEAD ON, O KING ETERNAL

Words by ERNEST W. SHURTLEFF
Music by HENRY T. SMART

LET ALL MORTAL FLESH KEEP SILENCE

Words from *The Liturgy of St. James*
Translated by GERARD MOULTRIE
17th Century French Carol

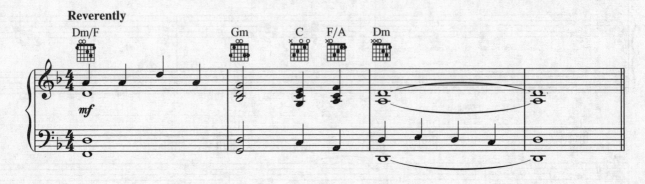

Let all mor - tal flesh keep si - lence, and with fear and
King of kings, yet flesh born of Mar - y, as of old on
Rank on rank the host of heav - en spreads its van - guard
At His feet the six - winged ser - aph, cher - u - bim with

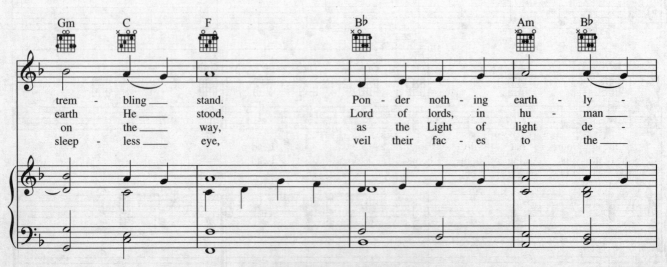

trem - bling stand. Pon - der noth - ing earth - ly -
earth He stood, Lord of lords, in hu - man
on the way, as the Light of light de -
sleep - less eye, veil their fac - es to the

THE LORD BLESS YOU AND KEEP YOU

Words and Music by
PETER C. LUTKIN

LOVE DIVINE, ALL LOVES EXCELLING

Words by CHARLES WESLEY
Music by JOHN ZUNDEL

Love di - vine, all loves ex - cel - ling,
Breathe, O breathe Thy lov - ing Spir - it
Come, al - might - y to de - liv - er,
Fin - ish then Thy new cre - a - tion;

Joy of heav'n, to earth come down;
In - to ev - 'ry trou - bled breast;
Let us all Thy life re - ceive;
Pure and spot - less let us be.

Fix in us Thy
Let us all in
Sud - den - ly re -
Let us see Thy

hum - ble dwell - ing, All Thy faith - ful mer - cies crown.
Thee in - her - it, Let us find that prom - ised rest.
turn and nev - er, Nev - er - more Thy tem - ples leave.
great sal - va - tion Per - fect - ly re - stored in Thee;

LOVE LIFTED ME

Words by JAMES ROWE
Music by HOWARD E. SMITH

Moderately fast

I was sink - ing
All my heart to
Souls in dan - ger,

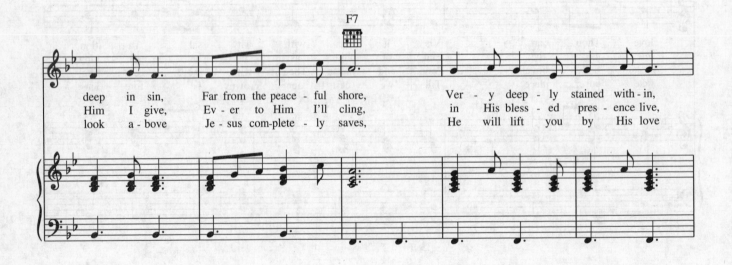

deep in sin, Far from the peace - ful shore, Ver - y deep - ly stained with - in,
Him I give, Ev - er to Him I'll cling, in His bless - ed pres - ence live,
look a - bove Je - sus com - plete - ly saves, He will lift you by His love

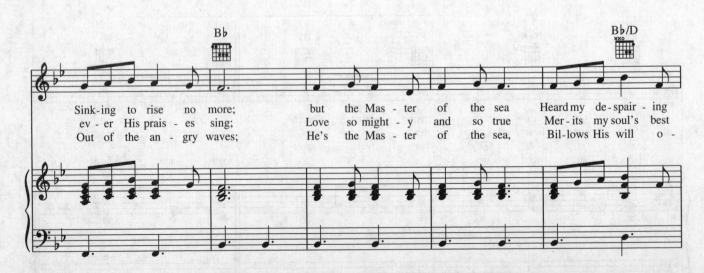

Sink - ing to rise no more; but the Mas - ter of the sea Heard my de - spair - ing
ev - er His prais - es sing; Love so might - y and so true Mer - its my soul's best
Out of the an - gry waves; He's the Mas - ter of the sea, Bil - lows His will o -

THE LOVE OF GOD

Words and Music by
FREDERICK M. LEHMAN

A MIGHTY FORTRESS IS OUR GOD

Words and Music by MARTIN LUTHER
Translated by FREDERICK H. HEDGE
Based on Psalm 46

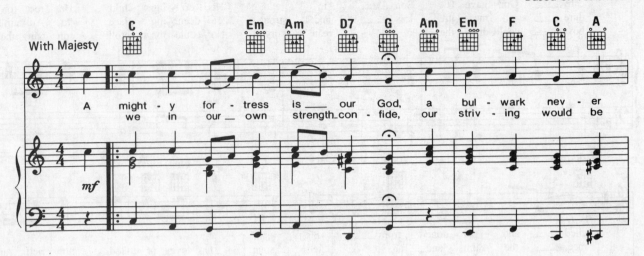

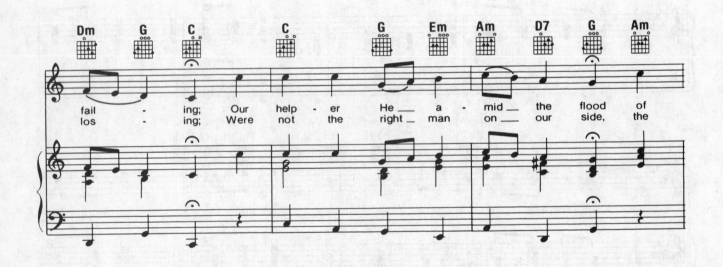

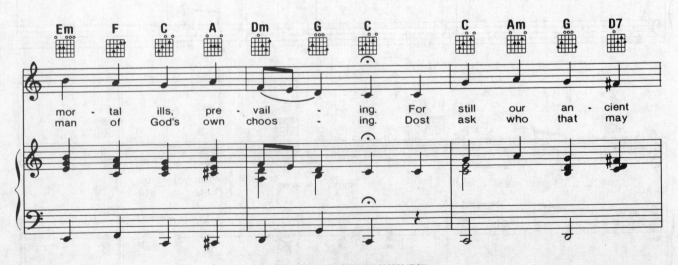

Additional Verses

3. And tho this world, with devils filled,
Should threaten to undo us;
We will not fear, for God hath willed
His truth to triumph through us;
The Prince of darkness grim,
We tremble not for him;
His rage we can endure,
For lo! His doom is sure,
One little word shall fell him.

4. That word above all earthly powers,
No thanks to them abideth,
The spirit and the gifts are ours
Through Him who with us sideth;
Let goods and kindred go,
This mortal life also;
The body they may kill;
God's truth abideth still,
His kingdom is forever.

MORE LOVE TO THEE

Words by ELIZABETH PAYSON PRENTISS
Music by WILLIAM H. DOANE

More love to Thee, O Christ,
Once earth-ly joy I craved,
Then shall my lat-est breath

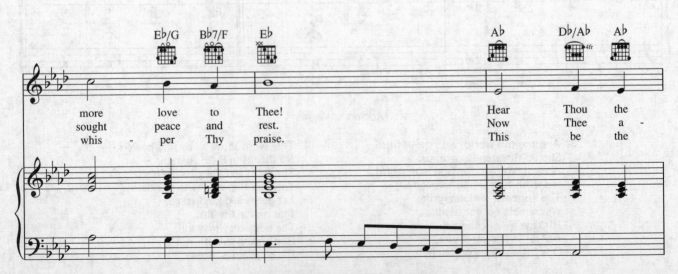

more love to Thee!
sought peace and rest.
whis-per and Thy praise.

Hear Thou the
Now Thee a-
This be the

MUST JESUS BEAR THE CROSS ALONE

Words by THOMAS SHEPHERD
Music by GEORGE N. ALLEN

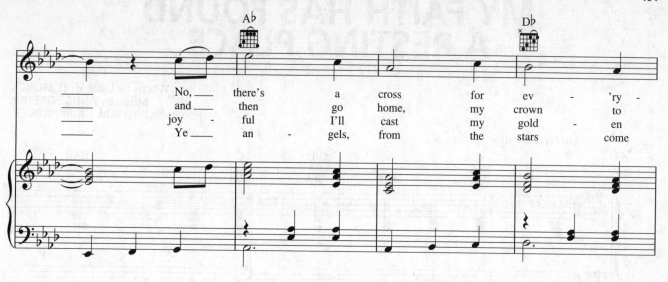

No, ___ there's a cross for ev - 'ry -
and ___ then go home, my crown to
joy - ful Ye ___ an - gels, cast from the stars gold - en come

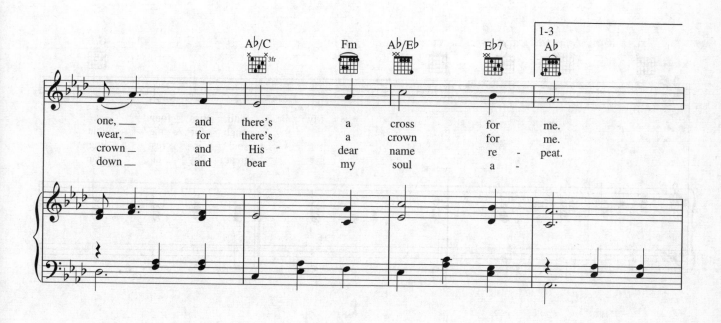

one, ___ and there's a cross for me.
wear, ___ and for there's a crown for me.
crown ___ and His dear name re - peat.
down ___ and bear my soul a -

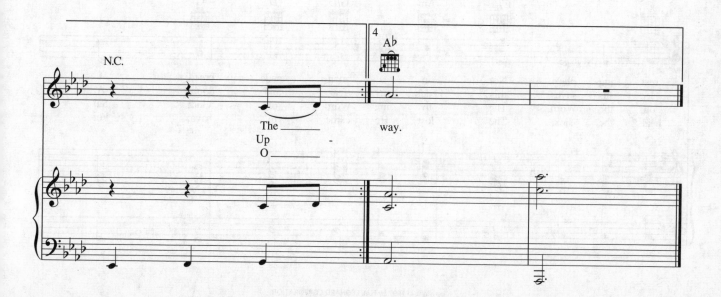

The ___ way.
Up -
O ___

MY FAITH HAS FOUND
A RESTING PLACE

Words by LIDIE H. EDMUNDS
Music by ANDRÉ GRÉTRY
Arranged by WILLIAM J. KIRKPATRICK

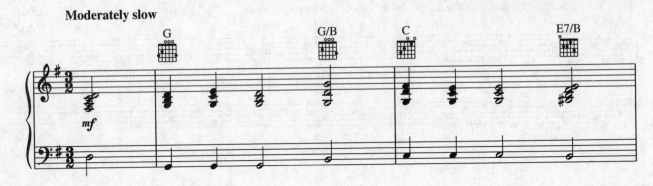

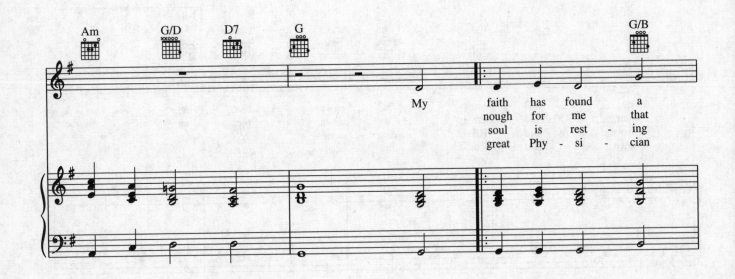

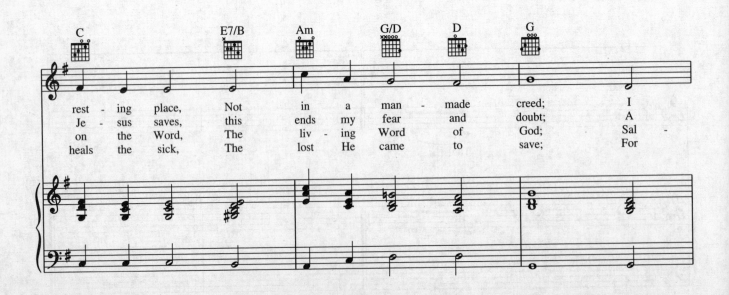

MY FAITH LOOKS UP TO THEE

Words by RAY PALMER
Music by LOWELL MASON

My faith looks up to Thee,
May Thy rich grace im - part
While life's dark maze I tread
When ends life's pass - ing dream,

Thou Lamb of Cal - va - ry, Sav - ior di -
Strength to my faint - ing heart, My zeal in -
And griefs a - round me spread, Be Thou my
When death's cold, threat - 'ning stream Shall o'er me

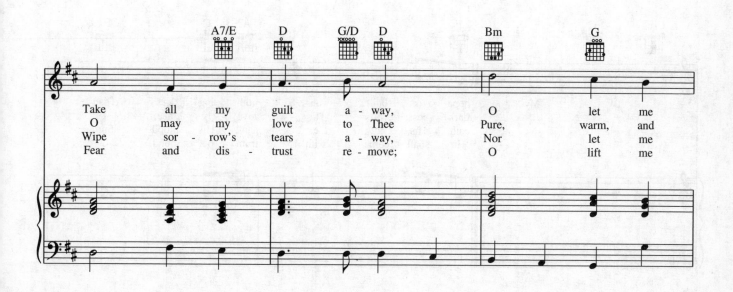

MY HOPE IS BUILT ON NOTHING LESS

Words by EDWARD MOTE
Music by WILLIAM B. BRADBURY

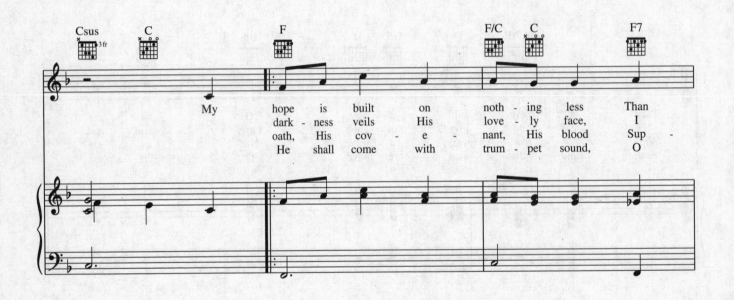

My hope is built on noth-ing less, Than
dark-ness veils on His love-ly face, I
oath, His cov-e-nant, His blood I Sup -
He shall come with trum-pet sound, O

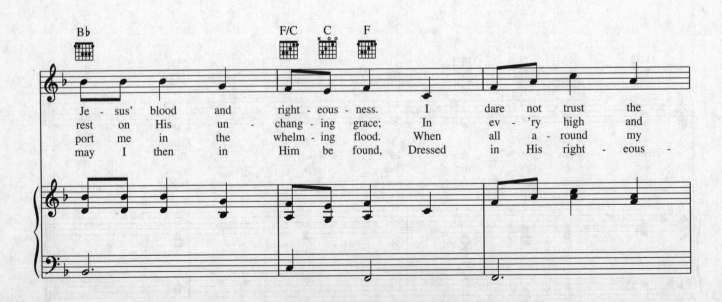

Je-sus' blood and right-eous-ness. I dare not trust the
rest on His un-chang-ing grace; In ev-'ry high and
port me in the whelm-ing flood. When all a-round my
may I then in Him be found, Dressed in His right-eous-

MY JESUS, I LOVE THEE

Words by WILLIAM R. FEATHERSTON
Music by ADONIRAM J. GORDON

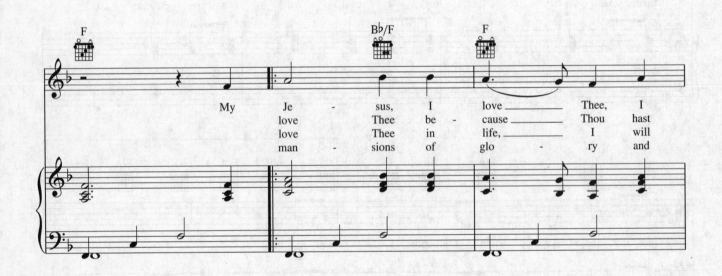

My Je - sus, I love _____ Thee, I
love Thee be - cause _____ Thou hast
love Thee in life, _____ I will
man - sions of glo - ry and

know Thou art mine. For Thee all the
first lov - ed me, and pur - chased my
love Thee in death, I'll praise Thee as a
end - less de - light, and ev - er

NEAR TO THE HEART OF GOD

Words and Music by
CLELAND B. McAFEE

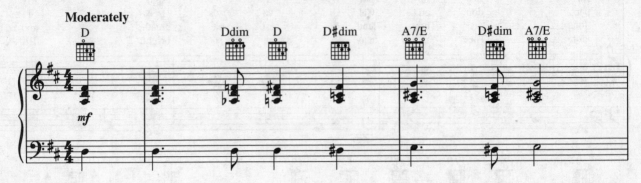

1. There is a place of
2. is a place of
3. is a place of

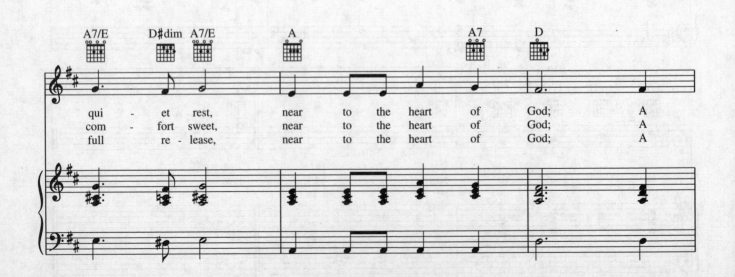

qui - et rest, near to the heart of God; A
com - fort sweet, near to the heart of God; A
full re - lease, near to the heart of God; A

NEARER, MY GOD, TO THEE

Words by SARAH F. ADAMS
Based on Genesis 28:10-22
Music by LOWELL MASON

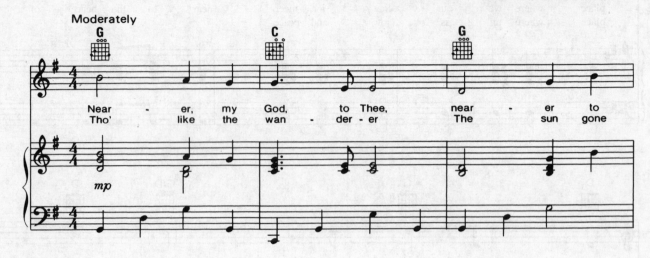

Near - er, my God, to Thee, near - er to
Tho' like the wan - der - er The sun gone

Thee! E'en though it be a cross
down, Dark - ness be o - ver me

that _____ rais - eth me. Still all my
My _____ rest a stone, Yet in my

song shall be, {
dreams I'd be, {
Near - er my God, to Thee.

Near - er, my God, to Thee, near - er to Thee!

3. Then with my waking tho'ts
   Bright with Thy praise,
   Out of my stony griefs
   Bethel I'll raise
   So by my woes to be,
   Nearer, my God, to Thee,
   Nearer, my God, to Thee,
   Nearer to Thee!

4. Or if on joyful wing,
   Cleaving the sky,
   Sun, moon, and stars forgot,
   Upwards I'll fly,
   Still all my song shall be,
   Nearer, my God, to Thee,
   Nearer, my God, to Thee,
   Nearer to Thee!

A NEW NAME IN GLORY

Words and Music by
C. AUSTIN MILES

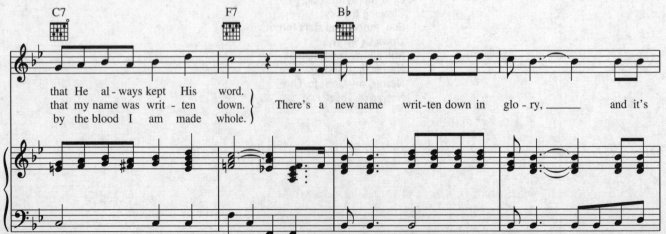

NOTHING BUT THE BLOOD

Words and Music by
ROBERT LOWRY

1. What can wash a -
2.,3. *(See additional verses)*

way my sin? Noth - ing but the blood of Je - sus;

What can make me whole a - gain? Noth - ing but the blood of

Refrain

C7   F   C   F

Je - sus. Oh, pre - cious is the flow

C7   F   C   F   C

That makes me white as snow; ___ No oth - er

F   1,2 C7   F   3 C7   F

fount I know, Noth-ing but the blood of Je - sus. Je - sus.

Additional Verses

2. **For my pardon this I see**
   Nothing but the blood of Jesus;
   For my cleansing this my plea
   Nothing but the blood of Jesus.
   Refrain

3. **Nothing can for sin atone**
   Nothing but the blood of Jesus;
   Naught of good that I have done
   Nothing but the blood of Jesus.
   Refrain

NOW THANK WE ALL OUR GOD

German Words by MARTIN RINKART
English Translation by CATHERINE WINKWORTH
Music by JOHANN CRÜGER

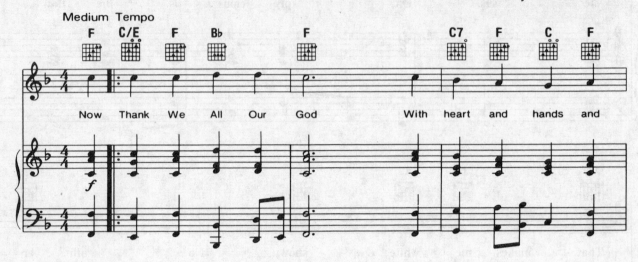

Now Thank We All Our God With heart and hands and

voic - es, Who won - drous things hath done, In

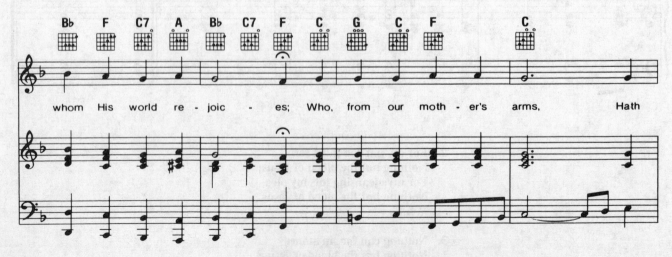

whom His world re - joic - es; Who, from our moth - er's arms, Hath

blessed us on our way With count - less gifts of love, And still is ours to - day. O more.

Additional Verses

2. (O) may this bounteous God
   Through all our life be near us,
   With ever joyful hearts
   And blessed peace to cheer us;
   And keep us in His grace,
   And guide us when perplexed,
   And free us from all ills,
   In this world and the next.

3. (All) praise and thanks to God
   The Father now be given,
   The Son and Him who reigns
   With them in highest heaven;
   The one eternal God,
   Whom earth and heav'n adore;
   For thus it was, is now,
   And shall be evermore.

O FOR A THOUSAND TONGUES TO SING

Words by CHARLES WESLEY
Music by CARL G. GLÄSER

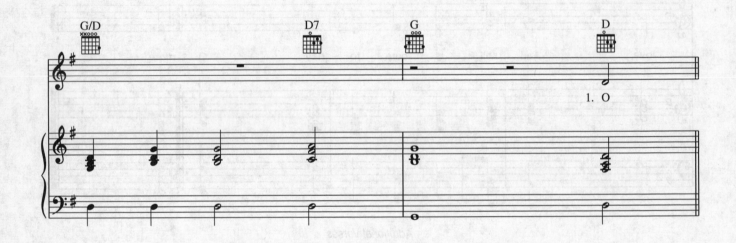

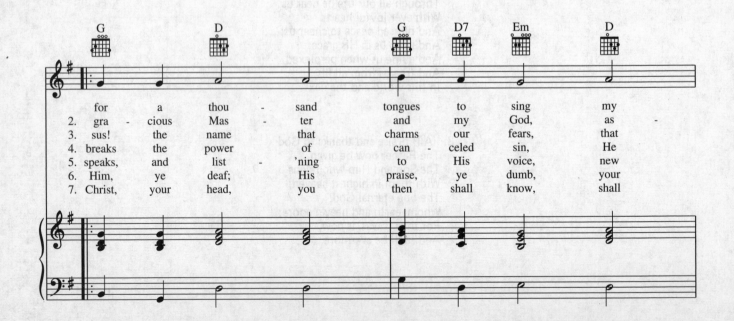

O GOD, OUR HELP IN AGES PAST

Words by ISAAC WATTS
Music by WILLIAM CROFT

O HOW I LOVE JESUS

Words by FREDERICK WHITFIELD
Traditional American Melody

There is a name ___ I love to hear, I
tells me of ___ a Sav - ior's love, who
tells me what ___ my Fa - ther hath in
tells of One ___ whose lov - ing heart can

love to sing ___ its worth; _____ It sounds like mu - sic
died to set ___ me free; _____ It tells me of ___ His
store for ev - 'ry day; _____ And though I tread ___ a
feel my deep - est woe, _____ Who in each sor - row

O JESUS, I HAVE PROMISED

Words by JOHN E. BODE
Music by ARTHUR H. MANN

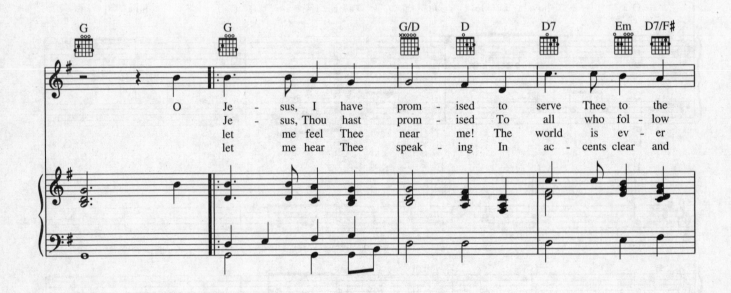

O Je - sus, I have prom - ised to serve Thee to the
Je - sus, Thou hast prom - ised To all who fol - low
let me feel Thee near me! The world is ev - er
let me hear Thee speak - ing In ac - cents clear and

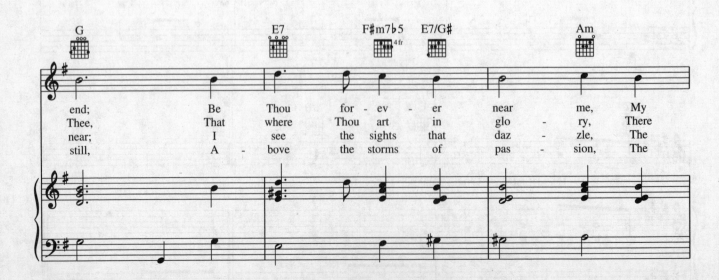

end; Be Thou for - ev - er near me, My
Thee, That where Thou art in glo - ry, There
near; A - bove the sights that daz - zle, The
still, A - bove the storms of pas - sion, The

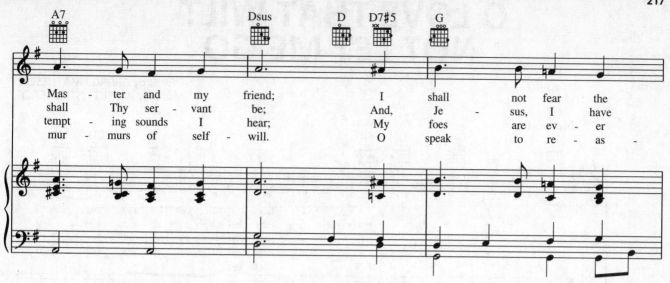

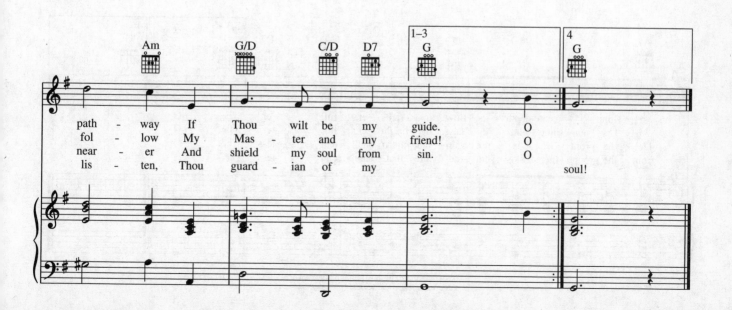

O LOVE THAT WILT
NOT LET ME GO

Words by GEORGE MATHESON
Music by ALBERT LISTER PEACE

PRAISE GOD, FROM WHOM ALL BLESSINGS FLOW

Words by THOMAS KEN
Music Attributed to LOUIS BOURGEOIS

O SACRED HEAD, NOW WOUNDED

Words by BERNARD OF CLAIRVAUX
Music by HANS LEO HASSLER

O WORSHIP THE KING

Words by ROBERT GRANT
Music attributed to JOHANN MICHAEL HAYDN
Arranged by WILLIAM GARDINER

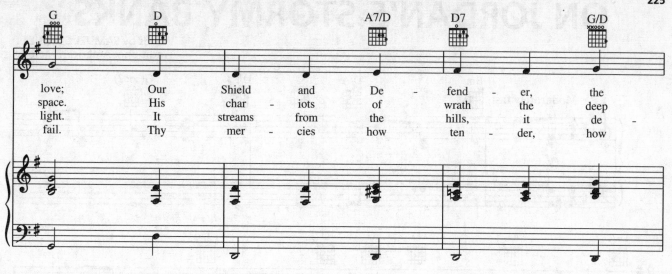

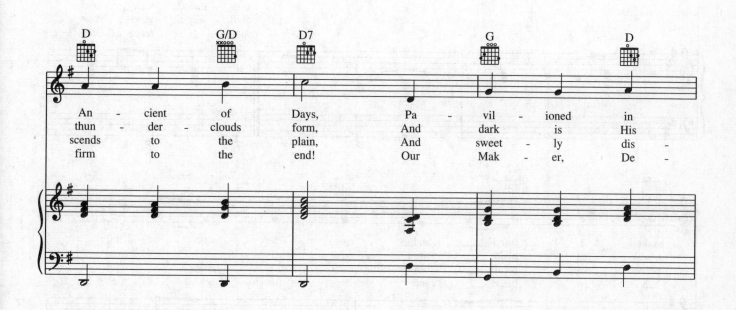

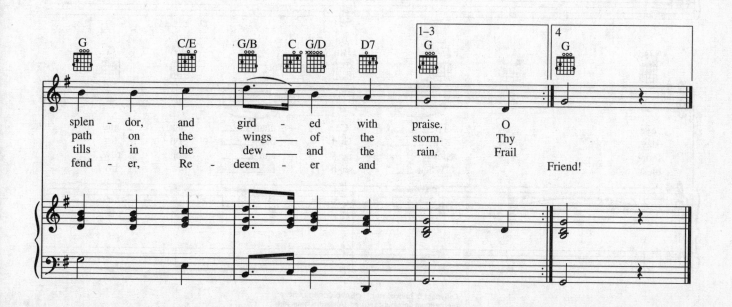

ON JORDAN'S STORMY BANKS

Words by SAMUEL STENNETT
Traditional American Melody

ONCE TO EVERY MAN AND NATION

Words by JAMES RUSSELL LOWELL
Music by THOMAS J. WILLIAMS

ONLY TRUST HIM

Words and Music by
JOHN H. STOCKTON

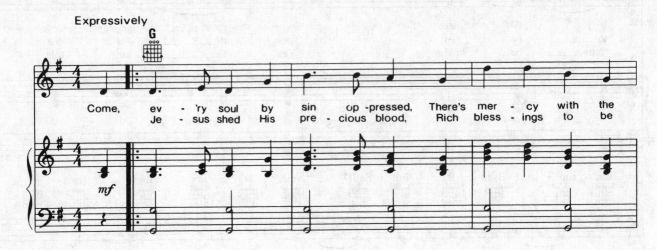

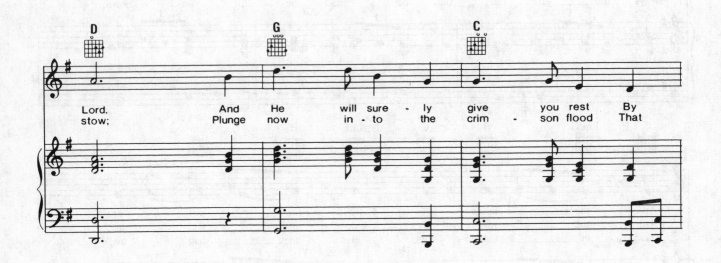

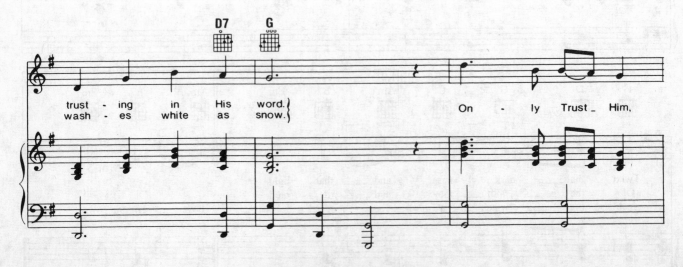

Only Trust Him, Only Trust Him now; He will save__you,

He will save you, He will save you now. For now.

3. Yes, Jesus is the truth, the way,
   That leads you into rest;
   Believe in Him without delay,
   And you are fully blest.

4. Come, then, and join this holy band,
   And on to glory go,
   To dwell in that celestial land,
   Where joys immortal flow.

OPEN MY EYES, THAT I MAY SEE

Words and Music by
CLARA H. SCOTT

O - pen my eyes, that I may see
O - pen my ears, that I may hear
O - pen my mouth and let me bear

glimps - es of truth Thou hast for me.
voic - es of truth Thou send - est clear;
glad - ly the warm truth ev - 'ry - where.

Place in my hands the won - der - ful key
and while the wave - notes fall on my ear,
O - pen my heart and let me pre - pare

PASS ME NOT, O GENTLE SAVIOR

Words by FANNY J. CROSBY
Music by WILLIAM H. DOANE

1. Pass me not, O gen-tle
2.-4. *(See additional verses)*

Sav - ior, hear my hum - ble cry;

While on oth - ers Thou art call - ing, do not pass me

Additional Verses

2. Let me at the throne of mercy find a sweet relief;
   Kneeling there in deep contrition, help my unbelief.
   Refrain

3. Trusting only in Thy merit, would I seek Thy face;
   Heal my wounded, broken spirit, save me by Thy grace.
   Refrain

4. Be the Spring of all my comfort, more than life to me;
   Not just here on earth beside me, but eternally.
   Refrain

PRAISE HIM! PRAISE HIM!

Words by FANNY J. CROSBY
Music by CHESTER G. ALLEN

Praise Him! Praise Him!
Praise Him! Praise Him!
Praise Him! Praise Him!

Je - sus, our bless - ed Re - deem - er! Sing, O
Je - sus, our bless - ed Re - deem - er! For our
Je - sus, our bless - ed Re - deem - er! Heav'n - ly

Earth, His won - der - ful love pro - claim!
sins He suf - fered and bled and died.
por - tals loud with ho - san - nas ring!

PRAISE, MY SOUL,
THE KING OF HEAVEN

Words by HENRY F. LYTE
Music by JOHN GOSS

PRAISE TO THE LORD, THE ALMIGHTY

Words by JOACHIM NEANDER
Translated by CATHERINE WINKWORTH
Music from *Erneuerten Gesangbuch*

REVIVE US AGAIN

Words by WILLIAM P. MacKAY
Music by JOHN J. HUSBAND

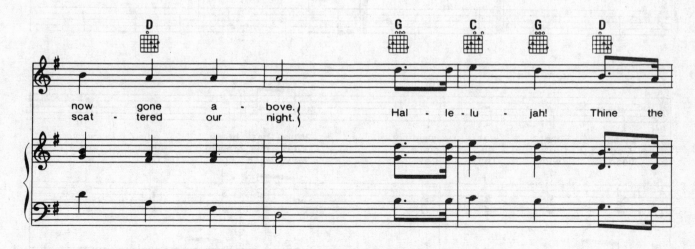

REDEEMED

Words by FANNY J. CROSBY
Music by WILLIAM J. KIRKPATRICK

REJOICE, THE LORD IS KING

Words by CHARLES WESLEY
Music by JOHN DARWALL

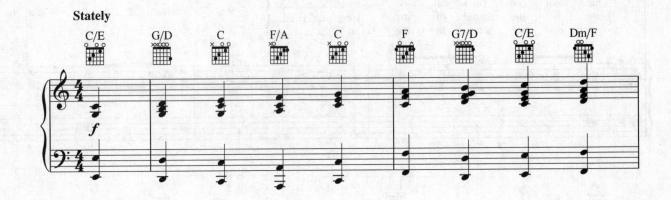

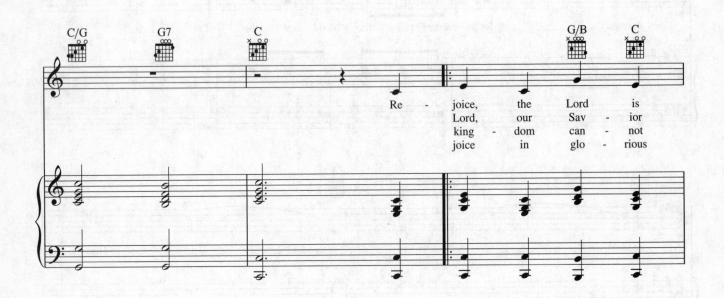

Re - joice, the Lord is
Lord, our Sav - ior
king - dom can - not
joice in glo - rious

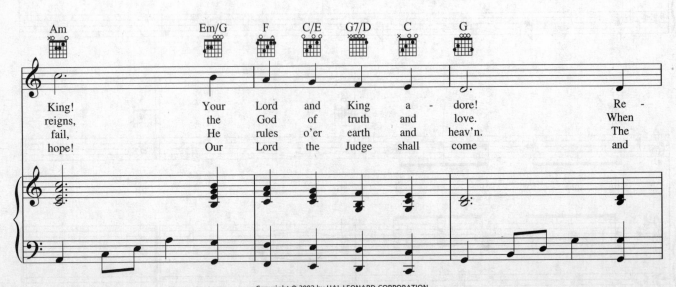

King! Your Lord and King a - dore! Re -
reigns, the God and truth and love. When
fail, He rules o'er earth and heav'n. The
hope! Our Lord the Judge shall come and

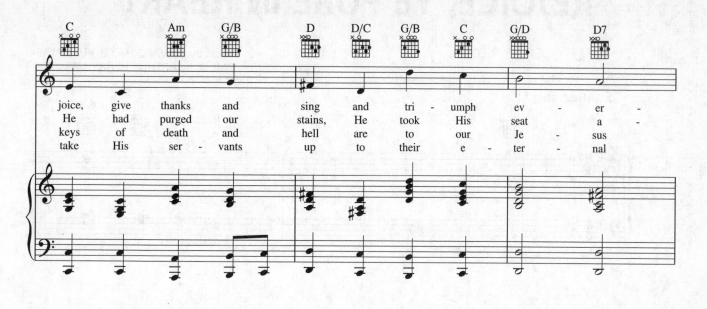

joice, give thanks and sing and tri - umph ev - er -
He had purged our stains, He took His seat a -
keys of death and hell are to our Je - sus
take His ser - vants up to their e - ter - nal

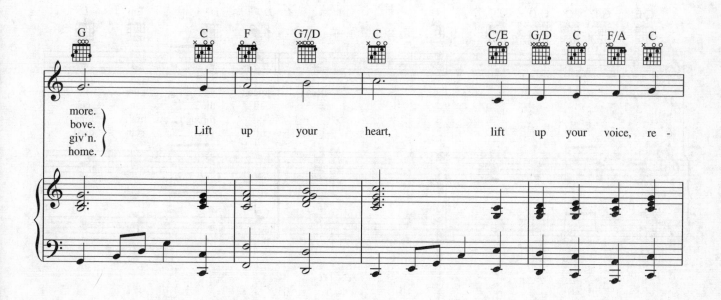

more.
bove.
giv'n.
home.

Lift up your heart, lift up your voice, re -

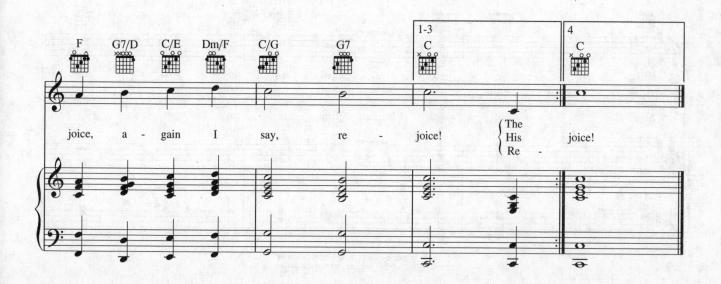

joice, a - gain I say, re - joice!

The
His joice!
Re -

REJOICE, YE PURE IN HEART

Words by EDWARD HAYES PLUMPTRE
Music by ARTHUR HENRY MESSITER

Re- joice, ye ___ pure in
all the ___ an- gel
on through ___ life's long

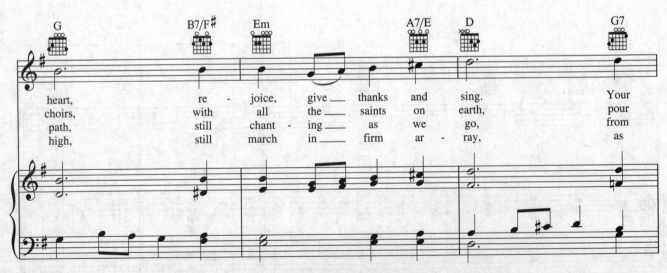

heart, re- joice, give ___ thanks and sing. Your
choirs, with all the ___ saints on earth, pour
path, still chant- ing ___ as we go, from
high, still march in ___ firm ar- ray, as

fes - tal ___ ban - ner wave ___ on ___ high, the cross of Christ your
out the ___ strains of joy ___ and ___ bliss, true rap - ture, no - blest
youth to ___ age, by night ___ and ___ day, in glad - ness and in
war - riors ___ through the dark - ness ___ toil till dawns the gold - en

King.
mirth!
woe.   Re - joice,   re - joice,   re -
day.

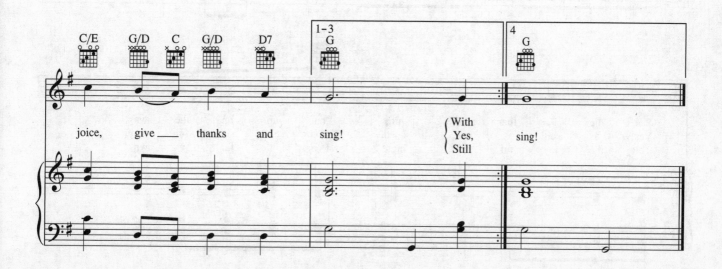

joice, give ___ thanks and sing!

With
Yes,   sing!
Still

RING THE BELLS OF HEAVEN

Words by WILLIAM O. CUSHING
Music by GEORGE F. ROOT

1. Ring the bells of heav - en! There is joy to - day,
2. Ring the bells of heav - en! There is joy to - day,
3. Ring the bells of heav - en! Spread the feast to - day!

For a soul, re - turn - ing from the wild!
For the wan - derer now is rec - on - ciled;
An - gels swell the glad tri - um - phant strain!

See, the Fa - ther meets him out up - on the way,
Yes, a soul is res - cued from his sin - ful way,
Tell the joy - ful tid - ings, Bear it far a - way!

SAVIOR, LIKE A SHEPHERD LEAD US

Words from *Hymns For The Young*
Attributed to DOROTHY A. THRUPP
Music by WILLIAM B. BRADBURY

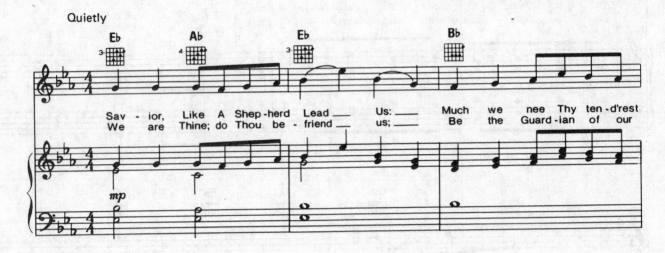

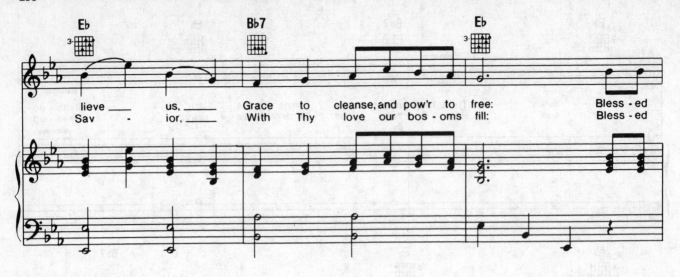

lieve ____ us, ____ Grace to cleanse, and pow'r to free: Bless-ed
Sav - ior, ____ With Thy love our bos-oms fill: Bless-ed

Je - sus, Bless-ed Je - sus, Ear - ly let us turn to Thee; Bless-ed
Je - sus, Bless-ed Je - sus, Thou hast loved us, love us still; Bless-ed

Fine   D.S. al Fine

Je - sus, Bless-ed Je - sus, Ear - ly let us turn to Thee.
Je - sus, Bless-ed Je - sus, Thou hast loved us, love us still.

ROCK OF AGES

Words by AUGUSTUS M. TOPLADY
Music by THOMAS HASTINGS

SEND THE LIGHT

Words and Music by
CHARLES H. GABRIEL

Additional Verses

2. We have heard the Macedonian call today:
   Send the light! Send the light!
   And a golden off'ring at the cross we lay:
   Send the light! Send the light!
   Refrain

3. Let us pray that grace may ev'rywhere abound:
   Send the light! Send the light!
   And a Christ-like spirit ev'rywhere be found:
   Send the light! Send the light!
   Refrain

4. Let us not grow weary in the work of love:
   Send the light! Send the light!
   Let us gather jewels for a crown above:
   Send the light! Send the light!
   Refrain

SINCE JESUS CAME INTO MY HEART

Words by RUFUS H. McDANIEL
Music by CHARLES H. GABRIEL

Additional Verses

3. There's a light in the valley of death now for me,
   Since Jesus came into my heart!
   And the gates of the city beyond I can see,
   Since Jesus came into my heart!
   Refrain

4. I shall go there to dwell in that city, I know,
   Since Jesus came into my heart!
   And I'm happy, so happy, as onward I go,
   Since Jesus came into my heart!
   Refrain

SPIRIT OF GOD, DESCEND UPON MY HEART

Words by GEORGE CROLY
Music by FREDERICK COOK ATKINSON

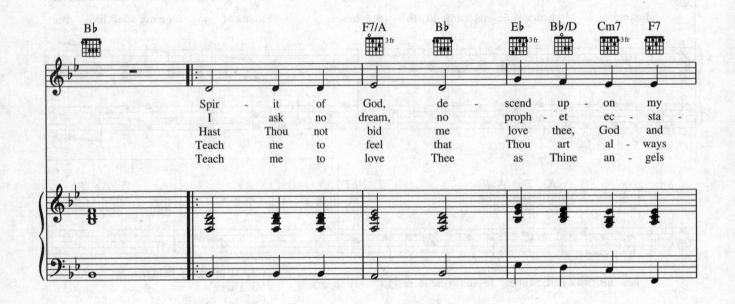

Spir - it of God, de - scend up - on my
I ask no dream, no proph - et ec - sta -
Hast Thou not bid me love thee, God and
Teach me to feel that Thou art al - ways

heart; wean it from earth; through
sies, no sud - den rend - ing
King? All, all thine own, soul,
nigh; teach me the strug - gles
love, one ho - ly pas - sion

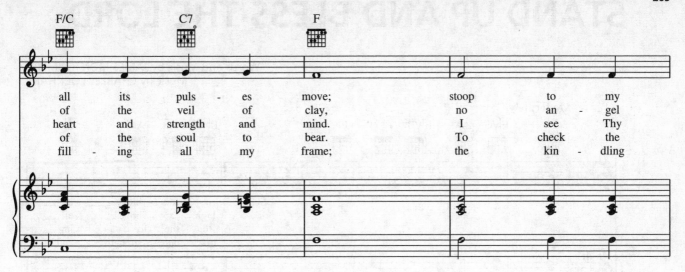

all its puls - es move; stoop to my
of the veil of clay, no an - gel
heart and strength and mind. I see Thy
fill - ing all my frame; the kin - dling

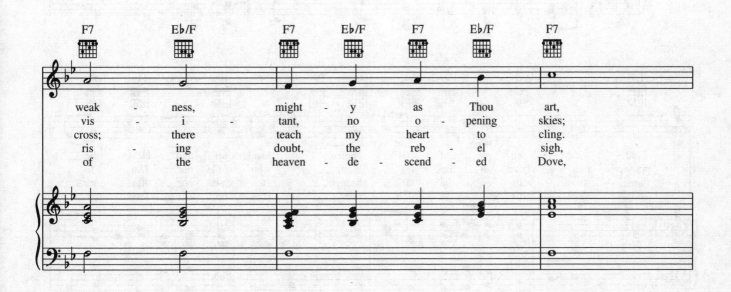

weak - ness, might - y as Thou art,
vis - i - tant, no o - pening skies;
cross; there teach my heart to cling.
ris - ing doubt, the heart reb - el sigh,
of the heaven - de - scend - ed Dove,

and make me love Thee as I ought to love.
but take the dim - ness of my soul a - way.
O let me seek Thee, and O let me find!
teach me the pa - tience of un - an - swered prayer.
my heart an al - tar, and Thy love the flame.

STAND UP AND BLESS THE LORD

Words and Music by JAMES MONTGOMERY
Music by CHARLES LOCKHART

TAKE MY LIFE AND LET IT BE

Words by FRANCES R. HAVERGAL
Music by HENRY A. CÉSAR MALAN

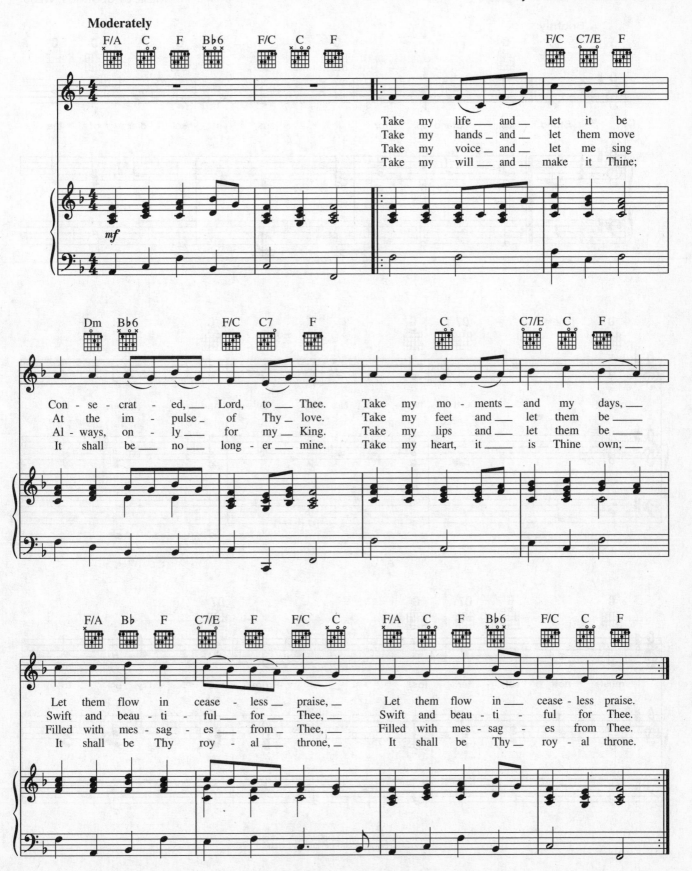

STAND UP, STAND UP FOR JESUS

Words by GEORGE DUFFIELD, JR.
Music by GEORGE J. WEBB

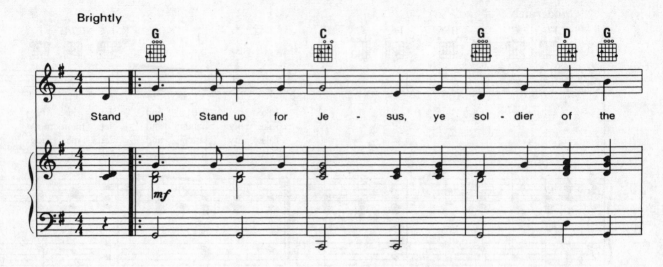

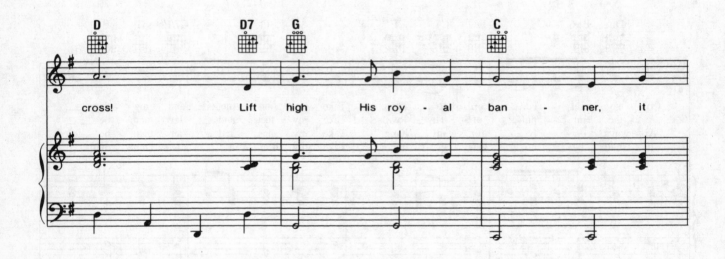

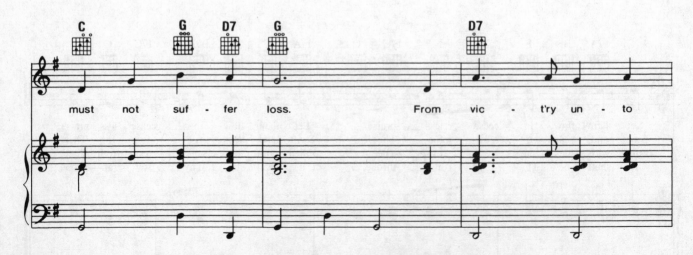

2. Stand up, stand up for Jesus,
The strife will not be long;
This day the noise of battle,
The next, the victor's song;
To him the overcometh,
A crown of life shall be;
He with the King of glory
Shall reign eternally.

STANDING ON THE PROMISES

Words and Music by
R. KELSO CARTER

1. Stand-ing on the prom-is-es of
2.-4. *(See additional verses)*

Christ my King, Thru e-ter-nal a-ges let His prais-es ring;

Glo-ry in the high-est, I will shout and sing, Stand-ing on the prom-is-es of

Additional Verses

2. **Standing on the promises that cannot fail,**
   When the howling storms of doubt and fear assail,
   By the living word of God I shall prevail,
   Standing on the promises of God.
   Refrain

3. **Standing on the promises of Christ the Lord,**
   Bound to Him eternally by love's strong cord,
   Overcoming daily with the Spirit's sword,
   Standing on the promises of God.
   Refrain

4. **Standing on the promises I cannot fall,**
   Listening ev'ry moment to the Spirit's call,
   Resting in my Savior as my all in all,
   Standing on the promises of God.
   Refrain

SWEET BY AND BY

Words by SANFORD FILLMORE BENNETT
Music by JOSEPH P. WEBSTER

SWEET HOUR OF PRAYER

Words by WILLIAM W. WALFORD
Music by WILLIAM B. BRADBURY

Sweet hour of prayer, sweet hour of prayer, that calls me from __ a

world of care And bids me at my Fa - ther's throne: Make all my wants and

2. (Sweet) hour of prayer,
Sweet hour of prayer,
thy wings shall my petition bear
To Him whose truth and faithfulness
engage the waiting soul to bless.
And since He bids me seek His face,
believe His word, and trust His grace,
I'll cast on Him my ev-'ry care
and wait for thee, sweet hour of prayer.

3. (Sweet) hour of prayer,
sweet hour of prayer,
may I thy consolation share
Till from Mount Pisgah's lofty height
I view my home and take my flight.
This robe of flesh I'll drop and rise
to seize the everlasting prize
And shout while passing through the air
farewell, farewel', sweet hour of prayer.

TAKE THE NAME OF JESUS WITH YOU

Words by LYDIA BAXTER
Music by WILLIAM H. DOANE

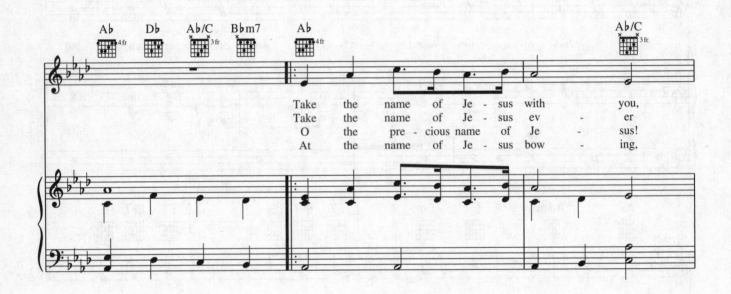

Take the name of Je-sus with you,
Take the name of Je-sus ev - er
O the pre-cious name of Je - sus!
At the name of Je-sus bow - ing,

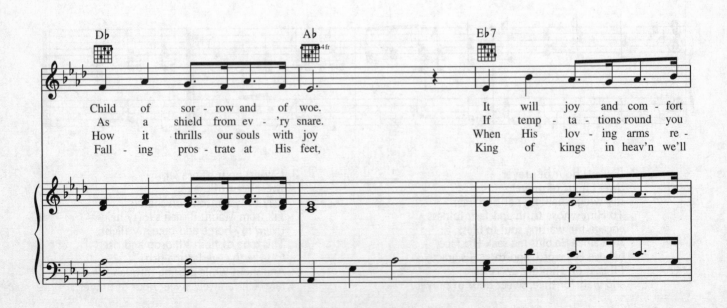

Child of sor-row and of woe.
As a shield from ev - 'ry snare.
How it thrills our souls with joy
Fall - ing pros-trate at His feet,

It will joy and com - fort
If temp-ta - tions round you
When His lov - ing arms re -
King of kings in heav'n we'll

THERE IS A FOUNTAIN

Words by WILLIAM COWPER
Traditional American Melody
Arranged by LOWELL MASON

Additional Verses

2. The dying thief rejoiced to see
That fountain in his day;
And there may I, though vile as he,
Wash all my sins away:...

3. Dear dying Lamb, Thy precious blood
Shall never lose its power,
Till all the ransomed Church of God
Be saved, to sin no more:...

4. E'er since by faith, I saw the stream
Thy flowing wounds supply,
Redeeming love has been my theme,
And shall be till I die:...

5. Then in a nobler, sweeter song,
I'll sing Thy power to save,
When this poor lisping, stamm'ring tongue
Lies silent in the grave. Amen.

THINE IS THE GLORY

Words by EDMOND LOUIS BUDRY
Music by GEORGE FRIDERIC HANDEL

Thine is the glo-ry, ris-en,___ con-quering Son.
Lo! Je-sus meets us, ris-en___ from the tomb.
No more we doubt Thee, glo-rious___ Prince of life!

End-less___ is the vic-t'ry Thou o'er death hast won.
Lov-ing-ly He greets us, scat-ters fear and gloom.
Life___ is___ nought with-out Thee; aid us in our strife.

'TIS SO SWEET TO TRUST IN JESUS

Words by LOUISA M.R. STEAD
Music by WILLIAM J. KIRKPATRICK

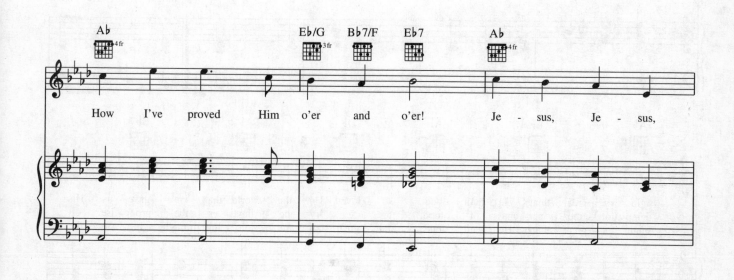

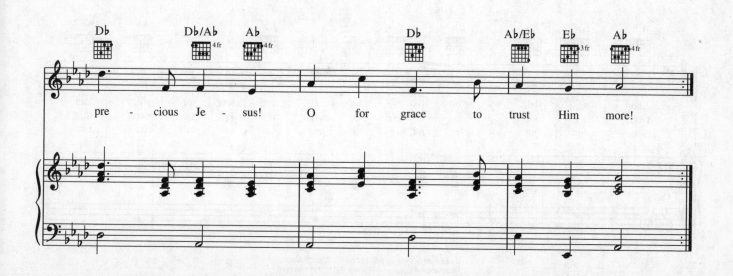

TO GOD BE THE GLORY

Words by FANNY J. CROSBY
Music by WILLIAM H. DOANE

To God be the
per - fect re -
things He hath

glo - ry, great things He hath done! so loved He the world that He gave us His
demp - tion, the pur - chase of blood, to ev - 'ry be - liev - er the prom - ise of
taught us, great things He hath done, and great our re - joic - ing through Je - sus the

Son, who yield - ed His life an a - tone - ment for sin, and
God; the vil - est of - fend - er who tru - ly be - lieves, that
Son; but pur - er and high - er and great - er will be our

TRUST AND OBEY

Words by JOHN H. SAMMIS
Music by DANIEL B. TOWNER

When we walk with the Lord in the light of His
shad - ow can rise, not a cloud in the
bur - den we bear, not a sor - row we
nev - er can prove the de - lights of His
fel - low - ship sweet we will sit at His

Word, what a glo - ry He sheds on our way! While we
skies, but His smile quick - ly drives it a - way. Not a
share, but our toil He doth rich - ly re - pay. Not a
love, un - til all on the al - tar we lay, for the
feet, or we'll walk by His side in the way. What He

TURN YOUR EYES UPON JESUS

Words and Music by
HELEN H. LEMMEL

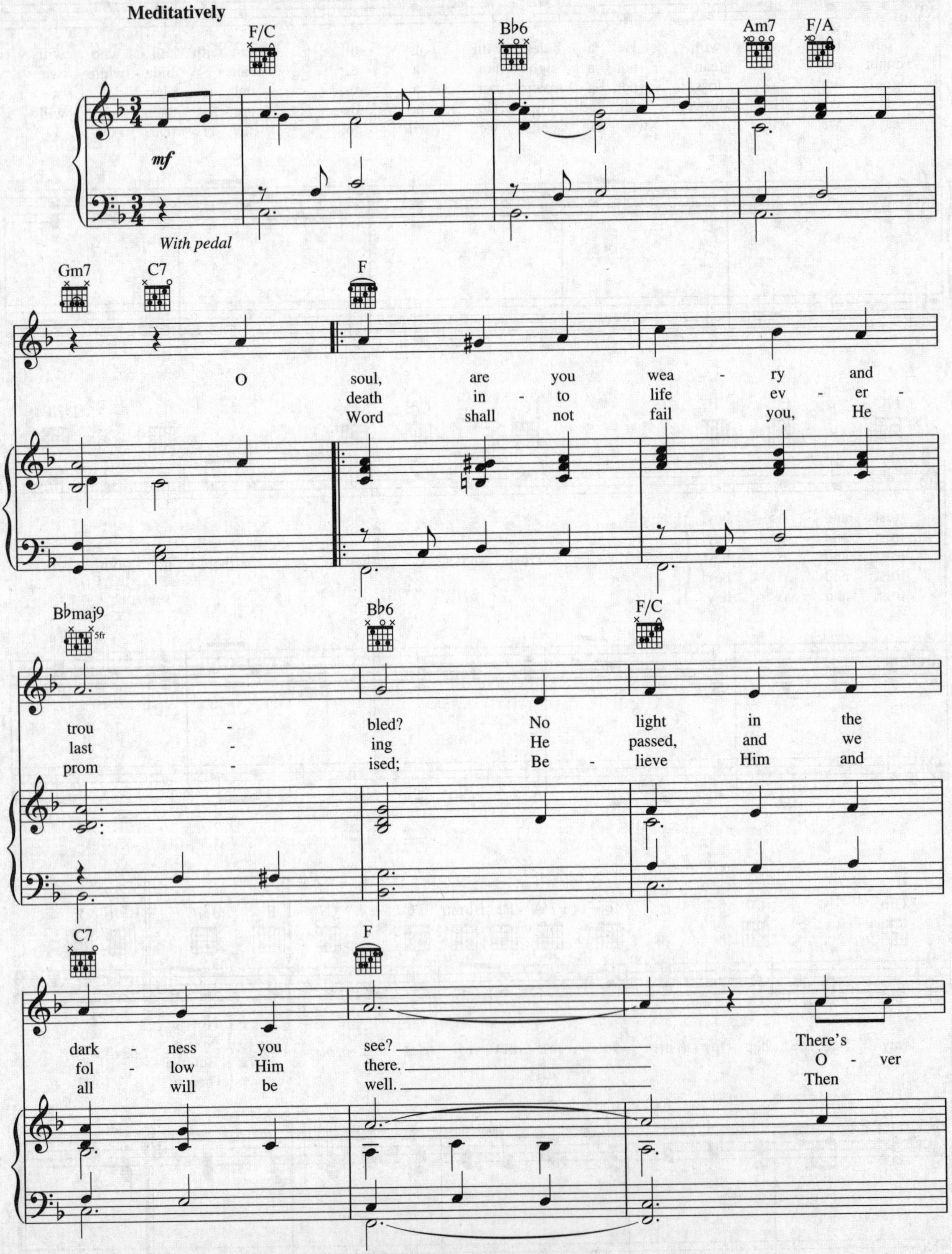

Meditatively

mf

With pedal

O soul, are you wea - ry and
death in - to life ev - er -

Word shall not fail you, He

trou - bled? No light in the
last - ing; He passed, and we
prom - ised; Be - lieve Him and

dark - ness you see? _____ There's
fol - low Him there. _____ O - ver
all will be well. _____ Then

WERE YOU THERE?

Traditional Spiritual
Harmony by CHARLES WINFRED DOUGLAS

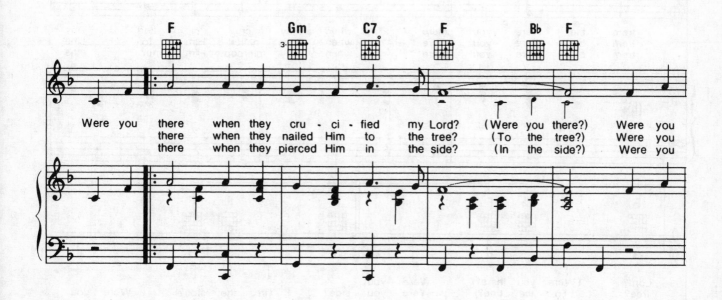

Were you there when they cru-ci-fied my Lord? (Were you there?) Were you
there when they nailed Him to the tree? (To the tree?) Were you
there when they pierced Him in the side? (In the side?) Were you

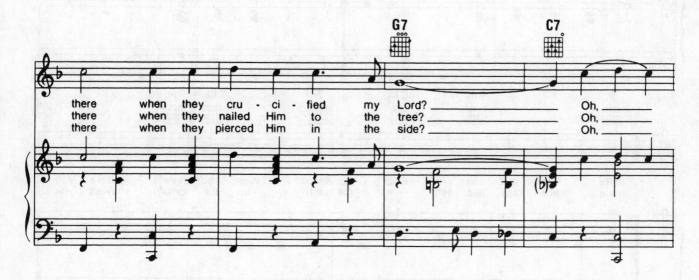

there when they cru-ci-fied my Lord? Oh,
there when they nailed Him to the tree? Oh,
there when they pierced Him in the side? Oh,

WE GATHER TOGETHER

Words from *Nederlandtsch Gedenckclanck*
Netherlands Folk Melody

WE'LL UNDERSTAND IT BETTER
BY AND BY

Words and Music by
CHARLES A. TINDLEY

Moderately slow

1. We are of - ten tossed and driv-en on the
2.-4. *(See additional verses)*

rest - less sea of time, Som - ber skies and howl - ing tem-pests oft suc - ceed a bright sun-shine, In that

land of per - fect day, when the mists have rolled a-way, We will un - der-stand it bet-ter by and

Additional Verses

2. We are often destitute of the things that life demands,
   Want of food and want of shelter, thirsty hills and barren lands,
   We are trusting in the Lord, and according to His word,
   We will understand it better by and by.
   Refrain

3. Trials dark on every hand, and we cannot understand,
   All the ways that God would lead us to that blessed Promised Land;
   But He guides us with His eye and we'll follow till we die,
   For we'll understand it better by and by.
   Refrain

4. Temptations, hidden snares often take us unawares,
   And our hearts are made to bleed for a thoughtless word or deed,
   And we wonder why the test when we try to do our best,
   But we'll understand it better by and by.
   Refrain

WHAT A FRIEND WE HAVE IN JESUS

Words by JOSEPH M. SCRIVEN
Music by CHARLES C. CONVERSE

ev - 'ry - thing to God in prayer. Oh, what peace we of - ten
take it to the Lord in prayer. Can we find a friend so
take it to the Lord in prayer. Do thy friends de - spise, for -

for - feit, oh, what need - less pain we bear, all be - cause we do not
faith - ful who will all our sor - rows share? Je - sus knows our ev - 'ry
sake thee? Take it to the Lord in prayer. In His arms He'll take and

car - ry ev - 'ry - thing to God in prayer.
weak - ness; take it to the Lord in prayer.
shield thee; thou will find a sol - ace there.

WHEN I SURVEY THE WONDROUS CROSS

Words by ISAAC WATTS
Music arranged by LOWELL MASON
Based on Plainsong

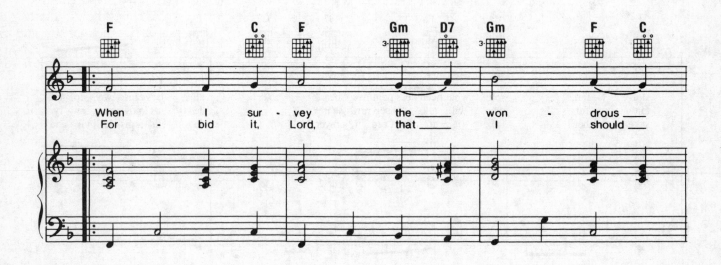

When I sur - vey the _____ won - drous _____
For - bid it, Lord, that _____ I should _____

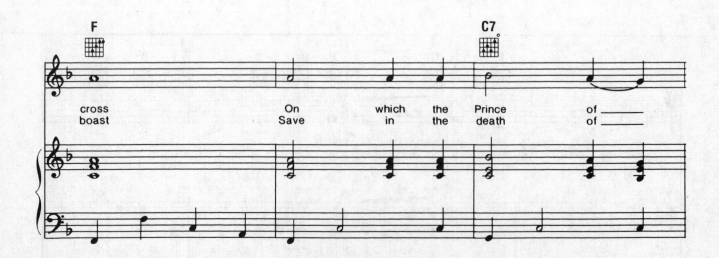

cross boast On which the Prince of _____
Save in the death of _____

3. See, from His head, His hands, His feet,
   Sorrow and love flow mingled down
   Did e'er such love and sorrow meet
   Or thorns compose so rich a crown.

4. Were the whole realm of nature mine,
   That were a present far too small.
   Love so amazing so divine,
   Demands my soul, my life, my all.

WHEN MORNING GILDS THE SKIES

Words from *Katholisches Gesangbuch*
Translated by EDWARD CASWALL
Music by JOSEPH BARNBY

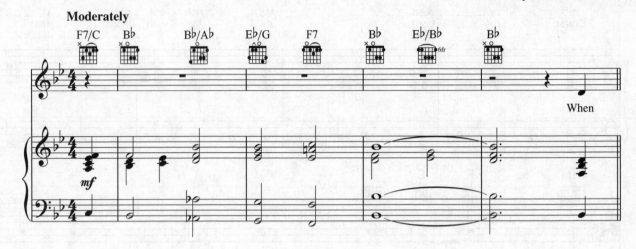

When

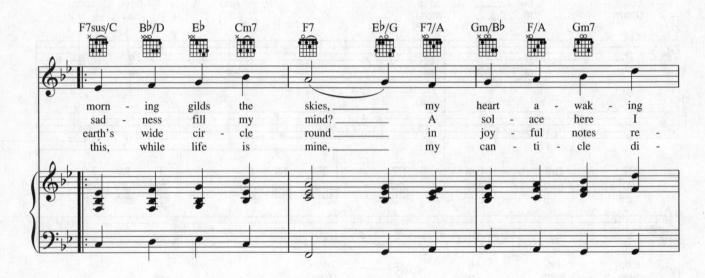

morn - ing gilds the skies, _____ my heart a - wak - ing
sad - ness fill my mind? _____ A sol - ace here I
earth's wide cir - cle round _____ in joy - ful notes re -
this, while life is mine, _____ my can - ti - cle di -

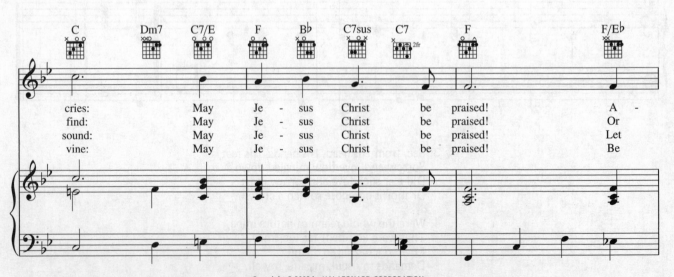

cries: May Je - sus Christ be praised! A -
find: May Je - sus Christ be praised! Or
sound: May Je - sus Christ be praised! Let
vine: May Je - sus Christ be praised! Be

WHEN WE ALL GET TO HEAVEN

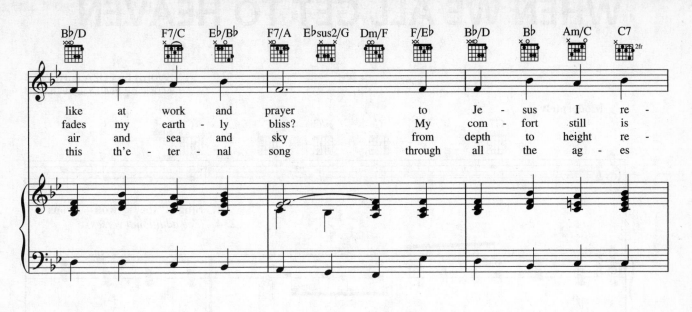

like   at   work   and   prayer   to   Je - sus   I   re -
fades   my   earth - ly   bliss?   My   com - fort   still   is
air   and   sea   and   sky   from   depth   to   height   re -
this   th'e - ter - nal   song   through all   the   ag - es

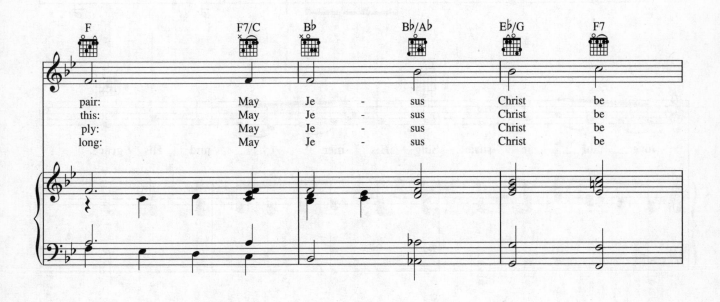

pair: May   Je - sus   Christ   be
this: May   Je - sus   Christ   be
ply: May   Je - sus   Christ   be
long: May   Je - sus   Christ   be

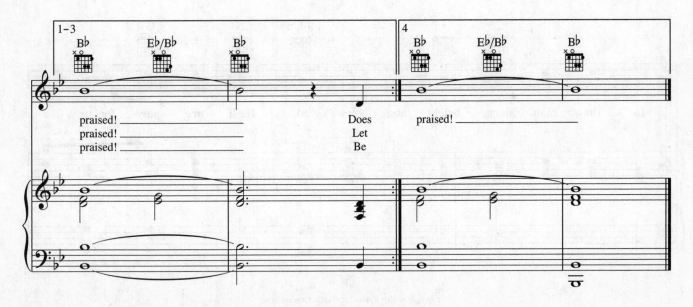

praised! _____   Does   praised! _____
praised! _____   Let
praised! _____   Be

WHEN WE ALL GET TO HEAVEN

Words by ELIZA E. HEWITT
Music by EMILY D. WILSON

1. Sing the won-drous
2.-4. *(See additional verses)*

love __ of __ Je - sus; Sing His mer - cy __ and His grace.

In the man - sions, bright and bless - ed, He'll pre - pare for us a

place. When we all get to heav – en, What a day of re-joic – ing that will be! When we all see Je – sus, We'll sing and shout the vic – to – ry. ry.

Additional Verses

2. **While we walk the pilgrim pathway,**
   Clouds will overspread the sky;
   But when trav'ling days are over,
   Not a shadow, not a sigh!
   Refrain

3. **Let us then be true and faithful,**
   Trusting, serving ev'ryday.
   Just one glimpse of Him in glory
   Will the toils of life repay.
   Refrain

4. **Onward to the prize before us!**
   Soon His beauty we'll behold.
   Soon the pearly gates will open;
   We shall tread the streets of gold.
   Refrain

WHISPERING HOPE

Words and Music by
ALICE HAWTHORNE

gen - tle per - sua - sion,
deep - en - ing dark - ness

whis - pers her com - fort - ing word.____
bright - en the glim - mer - ing star?____

Wait till the dark - ness is o - ver.
Then when the night is up - on us,

Wait till the tem - pest is done.____
why should the heart sink a - way?____

WHITER THAN SNOW

Words by JAMES L. NICHOLSON
Music by WILLIAM G. FISCHER

1. Lord Je - sus, I long to be per - fect - ly whole; I
2.-4. *(See additional verses)*

want Thee for - ev - er to live in my soul, Break

down ev - ery i - dol, cast out ev - 'ry foe; Now

Additional Verses

2. Lord Jesus, look down from Thy throne in the skies,
   And help me to make a complete sacrifice;
   I give up myself, and whatever I know,
   Now wash me and I shall be whiter than snow.
   Refrain

3. Lord Jesus, for this I most humbly entreat,
   I wait, blessed Lord, at Thy crucified feet;
   By faith, for my cleansing I see Thy blood flow,
   Now wash me and I shall be whiter than snow.
   Refrain

4. Lord Jesus, Thou seeest I patiently wait,
   Come now, and within me a new heart create;
   To those who have sought Thee, Thou never saidst "No,"
   Now wash me and I shall be whiter than snow.
   Refrain

WONDERFUL PEACE

Words by W.D. CORNELL
Music by W.G. COOPER

WONDERF WORDS OF LIFE

WONDERFUL WORDS OF LIFE

Words and Music by
PHILIP P. BLISS

WORK, FOR THE NIGHT IS COMING

Words by ANNIE L. COGHILL
Music by LOWELL MASON

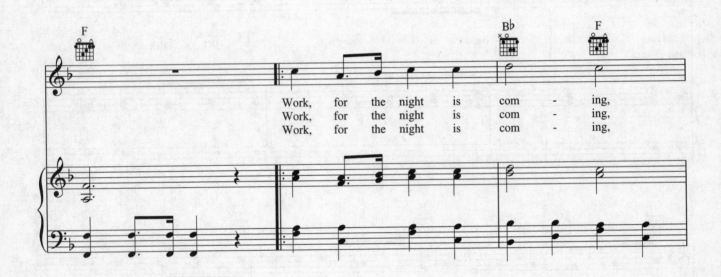

Work, for the night is com - ing,
Work, for the night is com - ing,
Work, for the night is com - ing,

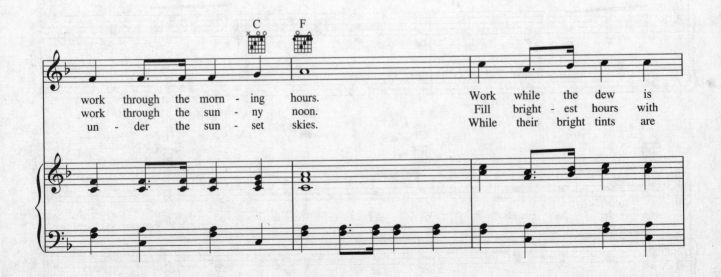

work through the morn - ing hours.
work through the sun - ny noon.
un - der the sun - set skies.

Work while the dew is
Fill bright - est hours with
While their bright tints are

WONDERFUL GRACE OF JESUS

Words and Music by
HALDOR LILLENAS